LIFE'S LESSONS

LIFE'S LESSONS

Illegitimi Non Carborundum:
Don't Let the Bastards Wear You Down

Dr. DAVID NOZICK

iUniverse, Inc.
Bloomington

LIFE'S LESSONS
Illegitimi Non Carborundum: Don't Let the Bastards Wear You Down

iUniverse books may be ordered through booksellers or by contacting:

iUniverse
1663 Liberty Drive
Bloomington, IN 47403
www.iuniverse.com
1-800-Authors (1-800-288-4677)

Because of the dynamic nature of the Internet, any web addresses or links contained in this book may have changed since publication and may no longer be valid. The views expressed in this work are solely those of the author and do not necessarily reflect the views of the publisher, and the publisher hereby disclaims any responsibility for them.

Any people depicted in stock imagery provided by Thinkstock are models, and such images are being used for illustrative purposes only.
Certain stock imagery © Thinkstock.

ISBN: 978-1-4759-1438-2 (sc)
ISBN: 978-1-4759-1440-5 (hc)
ISBN: 978-1-4759-1439-9 (ebk)

Library of Congress Control Number: 2012907269

Printed in the United States of America

iUniverse rev. date: 05/15/2012

CONTENTS

DEDICATION

This manuscript is dedicated to my parents, Roy and Mary Levi Nozick, who gave me the values of compassion, care for my fellow man and having personal responsibility to make a difference in the world. To my five children, all free spirits who move to their own beats, live exemplary lives and hopefully are aware of my boundless love for them.

To my five blessings, my grandchildren, who make Zaidi's life more meaningful and to whom the baton is about to be passed to make this a better world.

To my friends and family, who have been there for me through this adventurous and sometimes difficult journey called life, I thank for support and love.

To Mo, my mentor who taught me the real lessons of life, who took me under his wings and started me down the rich and fulfilling road of Clinical Psychology, I thank him from the bottom of my heart knowing that somewhere up there he has a **protégée** under his wings.

ACKNOWLEDGEMENTS

This book outlines a chain of events that occurred in my life. Others may disagree on its interpretation. However, limited by my memory, I have tried to be true to the facts. Any error or omission is solely my responsibility. The names of clients and some professional associates have been altered to maintain confidentiality.

Gail, Sarah, Lynn, Stanley, Josseline, who shared in the manuscript, I thank for patience and understanding. For the many phone calls, the reading and re-reading of the manuscript, the countless hours of support and encouragement, I truly appreciate each one of you.

My daughters-in-law, Nicole and Michelle, who with love and sensitivity supported this work, I thank for their professionalism and, more importantly, for being the foundation for my sons, Jason and Daniel, and my grandchildren. I also want to thank my sons Jason, Greg and Daniel for allowing me the privilege of being their father and, despite my fall from grace, who understood and forgave my transgressions and welcomed me back into their lives.

I thank my siblings, Stanley and Jo-Anne, who despite our dysfunctional family have been there for me with love, legal and editorial advice when I chose to open our family secrets to the world.

Jeanne, who has been a lifetime friend and colleague, I thank for her comments, support and more importantly for being there for me as I navigated various ports in the world.

I thank Sue Jennings, whose seminar and courage to tell her story inspired and motivated me to do likewise. Her insightful comments, criticism and critique made this a better book.

Michael, my teacher, thank you for helping me overcome my deficiencies in basic English grammar, spelling and in use of *The Canadian Press Stylebook* writing guide. Your advice and support made this book a reality.

I thank my friend Lou, who helped design the front cover and whose friendship means a lot to me.

To my new friend Bill Fairbairn, whose journalistic and editorial expertise added to the manuscript in so many ways, I thank for his support and professionalism.

INTRODUCTION

T. S. Eliot's Little Gidding
From The Four Quartets

"What we call the beginning is often the end
And to make an end is to make a beginning.
The end is where we start from . . .
We shall not cease from exploration
And the end of all our exploring
Will be to arrive where we started
And know the place for the first time."

No life is perfect. Life consists of challenges and struggles that define identity and purpose. The purpose of this book is to educate others in the art of survival and in being true to their core identity. My story is about a chain of events I was helpless to stop when I temporarily lost contact with myself.

Without doubt I experienced many failures in life—not the least the breakdown of my marriage—but I always attempted to learn from my mistakes and become a better person.

The only certain outcome of life is death. Along the way there are countless opportunities for growth and enlightenment. With the end closer to the beginning come certain wisdom and the realization that life is precious and meaningful and that it is important to live one moment and one step at a time.

If I have learned anything it is to realize that despite many external demands a rewarding and successful life is achieved when one is faithful to one's values, dreams and goals.

In the words of my mentor Mo: "ILLEGITIMI NON CARBORUNDUM—Don't Let the Bastards Wear You Down."

xi

CHAPTER 1

THE END IS A BEGINNING

OCTOBER 15, 1987

With pain and sadness I leave my four-bedroom, two-storey brick home in an exclusive enclave.

Here I am, a forty-two year-old caring father of three teenage sons and by profession a clinical psychologist, drifting away like an empty vessel. I am rudderless and guilty after telling my best friend, confidante, lover and wife that I cheated on her. Anger_ of a magnitude neither of us had ever experienced_ poured forth from both our torn hearts. There is no way to stop the haemorrhaging. I stagger out of a home that took a lifetime to build and seconds to destroy.

I am now a small ship in an ocean without docket or port of call. What am I to do? How has my life deteriorated to such an extent?

As I leave home the setting sun radiates a soft, tranquil pink hue that contrasts with my pain and sadness. As I enter my grey battered station wagon with ripped seats and broken passenger door handle I turn the key and leave behind the world I have known. How did this happen?

I drive slowly and aimlessly measuring my next move. I take a mental inventory of many token friends, limited financial resources and no family harbour in the storm. I feel paralysed with fear and for the first time in my life totally alone.

I enter a far too brightly lit and well-known coffee house and order my usual extra large with milk. This normal daily ordering of coffee seems strange and out of step with the rhythm of my life. I look around and see some couples and note an elderly man with furrowed brow sitting alone in deep thought. I wonder if I will be like him in a couple of years.

I try to think clearly and stop my hands from shaking but there is no relief from my pain and sorrow. I decide to go to the only place I can think of. As I open the door to my office, I switch the lights on, climb the long wooden stairs and am startled by the hollow sound of my feet hitting the hardwood floor. Just the previous week I had decided to enter private practice as a clinical psychologist. Little did I know that the office I rented would soon become my sanctuary.

As I open the interior door, illuminated by a full moon, I feel strange and alone in this building where I had seen my last client only four short hours ago. I find the couch in my office and lie down. But rest and tranquility elude me.

As I try to sleep I feel helpless, inadequate and stripped of all pretences that had clothed my self-image. I am truly a lost soul.

As I lie awake I think back to the events that led to this despair.

Who am I? And how did I get here? What lessons in life did I neglect?

LIFE'S LESSON—Thought leads to feelings. Feelings lead to action. Think before you speak.

CHAPTER 2

LIFE IN A SMALL BOX

OCTOBER 15, 1957

As a boy growing up in the ethnic melting pot of North End Winnipeg I was naturally exposed to different cultures and activities that formed my identity. A simple walk around any block in North End Winnipeg, circa 1950s, was to taste and smell the wonderful aroma of cultures from West and Eastern Europe. It was hard to hide a smile while telling anyone not from "the Peg" of a young Jewish teenager playing ice hockey for the Canadian Ukrainian Athletic Club on the frozen tundra of the prairies in the middle of a winter storm on *Shabbos* (Saturday, the traditional day of rest for Orthodox Jews).

While I played for the Ukrainian club my brother was a star centre for the Canadian Polish Athletic Club. Winnipeg in the 1950s was a geographically isolated and friendly town where community was a way of life. No thought was given to picking up a stranger at a bus stop in the middle of winter, driving him to his destination even if it was nowhere near where one was going. Similarly, kids would shovel their neighbour's walk simply for the exercise.

My family lived in a modest four-bedroom home in the North End (not the rich South End). I shared a bedroom with my older brother, my princess sister having the privilege of having her own room. My brother and I were tightly bonded although there were limits. My father, somewhat a man's man, believed if you were going to fight, it should be done properly. Thus one day he came home with newly purchased professional boxing gloves for his young warriors. Anxious to win our father's approval we quickly donned the gloves and were soon hard at it. Within a microsecond

3

I was hit hard in the chest by my stronger and quicker opponent and fell to the ground gasping for breath. "Pump me, pump me," I yelled out. My brother's response was to get down on his knees and count 1 to 10. Only then did he try to help me.

Close friends told me that the Nozick brothers were known as the holy terrors of the neighbourhood (taking away the ladder of the neighbour fixing his roof was one example). For the most part we went to school, played sports night and day and managed to abide by most laws. One exception being the time my older brother decided to augment his door-to-door photography business by buying and keeping a pony in our backyard.

As a 12-year-old I often walked with my golf clubs several blocks to catch a streetcar to the nearest public golf course at West Kildonan. The club rule against reserving a tee-off time until you arrived at the golf course meant golf games took upwards of 10 hours to complete, all for the price of $1.75. Parents, without benefit of cell phone or blackberry to keep track, did not worry about my security when not arriving home until early evening. They taught you early that you had to depend on yourself to survive.

Another memory that comes to mind was my mother's need to find a bargain by dressing my brother and me identically. We wore the exact same yellow plaid shirts, blue overalls and penny loafers for the sake of parsimony. For years I thought I was an identical twin. It took the birth of my sister seven years later before my mother put to good use her considerable feminine attribute to dress up her daughter.

As a result of my mother's character trait my brother and I developed a strong bond like that of identical twins. Like all twins we faced a basic conflict. On one hand there was a strong need for closeness and on the other a strong need to individualize. Is it any wonder I chose a career of professional emotional caretaker and my brother chose to be a strong voice for others not capable of fighting for themselves?

Physically as a youth I was slightly paunchy, short in height with distinctive red cheeks that my neighbour's mother loved to pinch while calling me *Duddie* and telling me how cute I was. Secretly I wanted to punch her lights out.

As the middle child you soon learn that for some reasons there are fewer photos of you than your siblings and to get any attention from your parents you need to be useful. I soon realized that to receive any emotional sustenance I needed to be the perfect child. Being perfect meant not drawing attention to myself and doing what was asked without excessive needs or wants. I did this by being an excellent student, an outstanding athlete and a socially aware child. This routine I followed until in my forties I rebelled.

Childhood experiences impact upon adult psyche as clearly demonstrated by my lifetime habit of checking and re-checking the stove before I retire for the night. As a nine-year-old I had awakened one morning to find the kitchen walls blackened by soot and burnt particles from the fire the night before. Thus my seemingly neurotic and obsessive-compulsive behaviour is directly due to this event in my childhood.

As an adolescent, I attended St. John's High School, the same school where my parents met and fell in love many years earlier. St. John's, a public high school dominated by Jewish students, emptied on the Jewish High Holidays as both Jews and non-Jews celebrated each other's holidays.

As a high school student, I was an ordinary B+, always too busy with athletic pursuits and social activities to make the effort to become an A student. Possessing exemplary social skills, I became president of the Eskimo Chapter of AZA, B'nai Brith Youth Organization. I was actively involved in my best friend's successful campaign to become president of the school council. Similarly, I was accepted by the jocks as one of them. One of my most prized possessions is an orange J cloth letter, symbolic of excellence in school sports. No doubt my athletic pursuits helped me receive approval and love from my athletically gifted father

St. John's High School had the reputation of being *the* high school that many of Canada's brightest and talented students attended. One of my history teachers was to become premier of Manitoba and Governor-General of Canada. I thought this ambitious young teacher took his teaching too seriously. Other teachers had a more lasting impression including one well-known science teacher who assigned 10 pages of stupid printings for various transgressions. Mr. P, a math teacher who had an illustrious career with the Winnipeg School Division, was a marvellous educator who gave me a love of math I still enjoy today. Indeed, those grocery clerks subject to my game of estimating the total costs of goods, thereby handing them the exact dollar amount before it was calculated, should be silently cursing Mr. P's proficiency at teaching math.

From outside appearances I had it made it as a well-loved and popular student from a well-known Jewish family with solid middle class credentials. Although both my parents had enjoyed a rather limited formal education, they and traditionally other ethnic families encouraged their children to get a good education. I clearly understood that university was the only real option for me. My mother, in her senior years, proudly and liberally introduced her children as "my son the lawyer, my daughter the lawyer, my son the doctor."

Sometimes appearances were not what they seemed. Hidden below the surface unknown to other than family and close friends, was a chaotic and dysfunctional family life that propelled me into a lifetime role of emotional caretaker.

As the middle child with an older brother and younger sister I was thrust into the care-taking role at an early age because of circumstances beyond my control. My father, a stocky muscular man, was a dynamic and well-read agnostic and my mother, a breathtaking brunette beauty with a Marilyn Munroe figure, was raised in an orthodox Jewish home. They enjoyed a lifelong love affair. They were high school sweethearts who had raised three children and despite limits did their best to provide a loving and caring home.

Although passionately in love my father's frequent brushes with death from seven major heart attacks and my mother's fear of them resulted in a toxic environment where tension and fear ruled. There is not one major historical event of the times during which my father was not hospitalized. When asked where I was when President Kennedy died, I vividly recall watching the events of Dallas unfold on my father's television monitor in his room at the St. Boniface Hospital. My father's incapacity left me taking care of my mother, initiating my apprenticeship to a lifetime of care taking.

Although each of us children developed a unique bond with our parents our roles differed dramatically. My older brother was to play the role of protector and business partner; my sister did the "girly" thing with Mom by providing her with the basic necessities of life. I recall one incident when Mom resided at Lion's Manor, a nursing home for seniors in Winnipeg, and was not taking her medication. So as psychologist and mediator I consulted with the nurses and came up with a plan to hide the pills in what was Mom's favourite ice cream dessert. One scoop later, Mom exclaimed: "You're trying to trick me!" Calm was restored a few minutes later with the arrival of her number one son, the lawyer, who shouted: "Mom take the pills now!" She immediately did as told.

A few months before her death, I was visiting Mom and found her to be pensive, reflective and introspective. These were not her usual characteristics. Being the caretaker and sensitive son I realized something was wrong. "Mom what's bothering you?" After an awkward silence she began to tell me about her separation from my father three months before his death. For the first time in her life my 1960s era mother had asked my father penetrating questions about his business. My father, always proud and headstrong, left in a rage over how his wife could possibly question his business acumen. His untimely death three months later left an emotional scar on my mother that I proudly say I helped remove.

Upon my mother's death and in preparation for the Rabbi's eulogy we had an opportunity to discuss my mother's life with him. After spending an hour with us the Rabbi quite correctly remarked: "I think you are talking about three people, not one."

At that moment I decided to deliver my mother's eulogy.

"Dear Rabbi, family and friends,

We are here today to celebrate Mom's life and to recognize her spirit and the essence of who she was. Approximately six years ago, on the occasion of her 80th birthday, I reviewed her life. So I will not repeat it here. Suffice to say she was a gentle soul who showed incredible courage and inner strength to overcome the limitations she faced on a daily basis. But perhaps the most enduring and strongest quality Mom exhibited throughout her life was her survivor skills. Mom had been through countless personal struggles and somehow had been able to get through them until now.

Mom was a people person who talked to everyone. If Mom and Dad went on a trip it was Mom who made friends. Dad was the shy one.

To this day she was much loved by staff and friends at the Lion's Manor because she always took the time to say thanks when someone helped her. Mom was a woman who took great pride in her presentation. No matter the occasion she was elegantly dressed. A story was told that when Mom was in her forties she got all dolled up for a wedding, and was shocked when a 25-year-old man spent the whole evening flirting with her. *A story Dad would have loved to tell. That Mom had many secret admirers was well known to all of us in the family.*

Mom was a bargain hunter extraordinaire. How else to explain that for the first seven years of my life Stanley and I were dressed in identical outfits and I honestly thought he was my twin brother. It was that ability to stretch a dollar that served her well in tough times.

Throughout all she kept her spirit and devotion as a mother. As is often the case, only when we, her children, became parents and grandparents did we appreciate Mom's values and what she did for us. Mom had her own unique and special relationship with each of us. Stanley was her rock. He was the lawyer who made her feel safe. Jo-Anne was simply her caring daughter who did what daughters do best. I was her emotional confidante. We learned from Mom the art of compassion, of being a survivor in this sometimes cruel and tough world and most of all how to live a life with dignity and respect. Mom was considerate to the end. She waited for her children to come back from supper before she finally let go.

She was the proud grandmother of six wonderful, energetic and dynamic grandchildren, all with their own distinctive personalities, and two very special great grandchildren. All of them send their love and respect.

Despite her personal struggles she was always there for her three children.

In ending my remarks I would like to thank Stanley and Sandra for being there for Mom and for taking care of all the important details that made her life easier. Joanne and Michael thank you for the support you give Mom over the years.

> *Mom, rest in peace, G-d bless*
> *We love you!"*

My father, while physically short and stocky, was a larger than life figure to me. Intelligent, well read, he was highly energetic and thoroughly enjoyed a practical joke. A creative and outside-the-box thinker, he established *Goofy*, a retail novelty and joke store that soon became the store for someone looking for an unusual gift. Whoopee cushions and simulated turd were just some of the items sold. One of Dad's marketing ploys was dialling a joke. Simply by dialling a phone number, clients were able to listen to a joke, followed by an advertisement for the store.

My father organized a party to raise funds for The March of Dimes. It was the talk of the town. Guests were required to draw cards and then find their match for the night. At the time this was considered risqué behaviour. There were fines for sitting too long in a seat or not talking to your neighbour. For many years after my father was sought to organize parties.

My father was a big, small man, whom I idealized. Roy, the youngest of three brothers, was brought up by a stern, cold, calculating father and a caring mother who infused him with a mixture of socialism and capitalism that would take him a lifetime to integrate.

I recall one conversation I had with Dad, in which he encouraged me to become a millionaire and then work to help the poor. My father, a maverick, a rebel, a secular Jew, was ahead of his time in encouraging the wealthy to make society better by giving back. This attribute is not unfamiliar to Bill Gates and Warren Buffett in our current society.

My father inculcated me with integrity, justice and the belief one was capable of doing anything. He believed that to be a *somebody* you either had to be wealthy or have an outstanding education while in both cases giving back to your community.

Dad was an athlete known by his nickname *Lungie* for his booming voice while playing football, golf, soccer or baseball. What a wonderful legacy for his family! I know my father would "*kwell*" (take great pride) at the thought that two of his grandchildren became professional golfers. Sometimes I teased my brother, himself an exceptional athlete, by saying that the gift of athletics missed one generation in our family.

I would be remiss if I did not mention that my Dad was a big kid who enjoyed playing football with all the neighborhoods. Indeed, more often than not, my best friends would come calling not for me but for my Dad who was more than willing to drop everything for an impromptu football game.

I digress there. The story I want to tell is in Leible Herschfield's book *Jewish Athletes in Western Canada*. The story is that my father and one of his brothers were absent from a soccer game. The substitute player, more commonly called a ringer, announces himself to the referee as a Nozick only to be challenged: "Which one are you?" Yelling over to the coach "which one am I" thus blowing his cover.

Unfortunately, my father's ill health limited his activities and his untimely death at age 56 was a major loss to me. I had always sought my father's approval and love. In many ways he was a man of his time and not in tune with my more modern sensitivity and psychological make-up. My sister told me recently that my dad always wanted to write a book. This manuscript is in part an attempt to posthumously win his approval. I hope that had my father lived to read this manuscript he would be proud of what I say.

My professional ambition was fuelled in part by my desire to win my father's approval and love. Unknown to me it would prove to be a road that led to false happiness.

As a clinical psychologist reviewing my own family dynamics it is clear there are some fairly severe dysfunctional patterns within my family. My parents, despite their lifelong love affair, were unable to meet each other's emotional needs. Each of them had his or her own set of insecurities. My father internalized his stress, which ultimately led to his premature death. My mother's fears and anxiety regarding my father's health caused her to turn to me to meet her emotional needs, a task I was ill prepared to do as an adolescent. Attempting to meet my mother's insatiable emotional needs proved to be a major obstacle in overcoming my own emotional development.

LIFE'S LESSON—*Be true to yourself and your values and you will be rewarded with a life of peace and tranquillity.*

CHAPTER 3

———◆———

FALSE HAPPINESS

MAY 15, 1981

I won a competition to become the director of psychology at a major teaching hospital in Ottawa.

As a 36-year-old man, this was a tremendous accomplishment, only more so in that I had never worked a single day in a hospital setting. Somehow, I convinced the selection board that my clinical skills would be totally transferable to the hospital environment.

I wondered what I had done to myself as I reluctantly entered the hospital boardroom for my all-important interview. In front of me was the reflection of three men behind a glimmering 40-foot-long rosewood table. These decision makers would decide my fate.

I was invited to join them at the table and it became apparent that at some level they were welcoming me to the ship. I became more confident as the interview proceeded. Time seemed to stop. I became totally immersed.

Finally, the senior executive asked me the unusual question: "David, what are your hobbies?" At that instance, I knew I was among my peers.

I was on top of the world. I had fulfilled my highest professional dream and now occupied a demanding and respected position within the community. Little did I know there was nowhere to go from this lofty position but down.

By all appearance I was a successful executive who had it all: a beautiful wife, three active, healthy and fun-loving sons and all the joys that go with them. On the surface, there was balance in my life with many social contacts, a strong family bond and a multitude of interests and activities. Life inside the box was comfortable, secure and predictable.

As is the norm in a long relationship, my wife and I fell into a pattern of life that essentially revolved around the demands of our three sons and the need to maintain our position within the community. We were living the proverbial Canadian dream.

Or were we? I can't speak for my wife but, internally, I was feeling restless with a growing sense of frustration, anger, irritability and a general certain helplessness that was totally incongruent with my external world. Why? I do not know. As I said, by all appearances we were living the Canadian dream. But my inner world was full of uncertainty, anxiety and a layer of sadness that soaked my inner being. Outwardly, I maintained my role as a father, husband and a clinical psychologist but, despite my successes, I felt like a fraud. I had little or no understanding of who I was. It would take the eventual break-up of my marriage and five years of intensive psychotherapy before I would begin to understand who I was and what the meaning of that restlessness really was.

It seems that in my desire to please others—always the nice guy, always agreeable—I lost the *essence* of who I was. Living a life in which I would do almost anything to please others to receive their approval resulted in the loss of the most important thing a person can lose. I lost my inner core. I lost my ability to survive. It would be a long, arduous swim against the current of life before I truly found myself and reached inner harmony and peace.

It wasn't always so. At an earlier stage of my life I had known who I was and what I stood for.

LIFE'S LESSON—*Be true to your soul no matter what pressure there is to deviate.*

CHAPTER 4

GO WEST YOUNG MAN

SEPTEMBER 15, 1960

It would take a move to Tuxedo, a wealthy suburb in west-end Winnipeg near the picturesque Assiniboine Park, to really shake up the family. At the age of 15, I had entered university and the family had moved into a sprawling bungalow built around a grove of birch trees. The house was so large that it had three separate furnaces, one devoted to heating the garage in the frigid Winnipeg winters. My mother, who had a natural flair for fashion, hired a young interior decorator and he decided to make the living room a showpiece almost entirely in white including two white leather chairs and white carpeting contrasting with a pink loveseat. The room was furnished with the most ornate lamp featuring a gold leaf shade that resembled a Christmas tree. Today that lamp is safely stored for the next generation of Nozicks.

Truth be told, I was in the living room only once in my entire life and that was on the occasion of my engagement party some six years later. The house, despite its opulence and not unlike the house I occupied with my ex-wife prior to our divorce, was filled with bad karma, tension, unpleasantness and painful memories. Perhaps deep within me I had fought giving up my North End Winnipeg roots and values.

The move to Tuxedo proved to be unsettling for the family, but especially for my mother whose roots and stability also were in North End Winnipeg. The sophistication, wealth and expectations were simply too much for her to cope with and this resulted in a significant deterioration of her mental health.

On many occasions I found her leaving the home at odd hours of the evening after threatening never to return. Occasionally she found life's expectations simply too much and threatened to take her own life. One evening I found her with a plastic bag over her face. As her emotional caretaker I felt alone and ill equipped to deal with these traumatic incidents. No doubt my obsessive need to tie plastic bags three times before disposing of them is directly related to this incident.

My way of coping as an adolescent was to lose myself in sports and to be active socially. Somehow I always had a girlfriend and I carefully guarded family secrets. Today I would reach out to others for help. On one occasion my mother's behaviour was simply too hysterical from crying uncontrollably. We were unable to calm her down. The family situation was exacerbated by my father's precarious health making us fear that the next meltdown could bring on another heart attack or worse.

A hurried call to Aunt B, a woman of impeccable dress and comportment, known for her toughness and ability to handle difficult situations, resulted in their setting off to hospital. My mother, a natural brunette beauty, prepared herself, as she would any time she went out in public. She applied her make-up and chose her clothes to perfection. My aunt, responding to the family emergency, went as she was. She later told us the emergency doctor mistakenly thought she was the patient in need of help. I will leave the interpretation of this event to the reader. However, on other occasions working in the mental health system, I have seen the same thing. As a student at a psychiatric hospital in Winnipeg I witnessed a distinguished psychiatrist interview a paranoid schizophrenic patient in front of hundreds of doctors and at the same time try to reassure the patient that the audience would maintain her confidentiality.

Arriving at the University of Manitoba science class in 1962, I was totally unprepared for the freedom and the rigours of academic life. I recall sitting in a large amphitheatre totally confused and in shock when the physics professor started to discuss a formula using concepts of basic trigonometry. Unfortunately for us we had not yet taken trigonometry in our mathematics class. My mark of 36 in the Christmas exam was an accurate reflection of my academic performance at that time.

In addition to dealing with the academic aspect of life I immersed myself in the social aspects of university. I became pledge captain to a fraternity my brother belonged to. Then I *de-pledged* to join a group that formed its own fraternity. This group became the GDIs (G-d Damn

Independents) comprised of boys later to become men who thought outside the box and become leaders in society.

University was also when I became aware of the blessings of good health. Suddenly one spring evening, when I was in the middle of my final third-year exams, I was hit with excruciating abdominal pain. Having recently been the victim of a kidney stone that would not pass, I can state categorically the abdominal pain was a hundred times more intense than anything I had ever experienced before. It felt like a knife was cutting through my stomach without the benefit of an anaesthetic. Taken to the hospital by ambulance I was wheeled into the operating room where a prominent surgeon operated. I later learned I had a congenital condition called Meckel's diverticulum. Essentially it is a small bulge in the small intestine present at birth and affecting about 2 per cent of the population and males more frequently than females.

In my case the symptom was intestinal obstruction. The only treatment is surgery, consisting of a resection of the affected portion of the bowel. On a lighter note, pun intended, the operation has similar results as gastric by-pass surgery. My older brother had a similar experience when he was two and recovered completely. Ironically, I have recently been requested to psychologically clear gastric by-pass patients before their surgeon consider them for surgery.

Unfortunately my recovery did not go well. Five days after surgery I went to the washroom and started haemorrhaging. Once again I was taken to the hospital receiving numerous blood transfusions that saved my life.

Things seemed to be going better until several months later when I once again experienced abdominal pain that made the other incident pale in comparison. Two injections of morphine did little to dull the intense pain. Subsequent surgery revealed I had an adhesion that was strangling my bowel line. Without follow-up surgery I would have died.

Despite the seriousness of these events two other related stories warrant telling. After deferring all my third-year exams because of the surgery and writing the supplemental exams, I received a mark of 96 in calculus. When I met the professor to receive my mark, he remarked: "What were you doing all year?"

The second incident occurred many years later when my mother was fighting for her life in the ICU at the Miscercordia Hospital in Winnipeg. As befits my personality I had befriended the doctor in charge. During the weeks my mother was hospitalized the doctor and I talked about the meaning of life and death. Strange how the closeness of death affords you the opportunity to understand what is important in life. As circumstances happened, I bumped into the surgeon who had done my surgery some 25 years earlier. I told him how well he looked and asked if he remembered my surgery. When he replied: "I did a Meckel's diverticulum on you." I shot back: "The only reason you remember is you butchered me."

After a good laugh he tried to convince me to return to Winnipeg to practise psychology. Later I met the ICU doctor who was upset with me because I did not tell *him* how good he looked.

Having learned of my troubled family background and my strong caretaker role it will not surprise readers to learn that as a young man I was considering a career as a physician and as a psychiatrist. To be a Jewish *mensch* (honourable man) in Winnipeg in the 1960s meant a lot of things to different people. To my late father it meant you had the choice of being highly educated or rich.

For years I took this as a prescription for success while failing to question or filter the advice of a man I respected and loved. Given this advice, together with my need to meet my mother's emotional needs, is it any wonder I pursued a career in medicine and psychiatry? With my excellent study skills, reasonable intelligence and a fierce determination to succeed, I was headed for a career in medicine when suddenly my life took a dramatic turn. I decided on the strength of two psychology courses not to go to medical school but to enter the field of psychology.

This sudden turn of events led me to the most incredibly fulfilling, rewarding and exciting career. I was privileged to counsel thousands of outstanding individuals and families. Of note to those of you who have sought therapy may I say that it is only the brave and strong that choose to face their demons. It is only by recognizing, experiencing and understanding our emotional fears that we can hope to grow and move forward in our lives.

What followed the turmoil of adolescence was a reasonably tranquil period in which I acquiesced to social norms, followed the path of least resistance, obtained higher education, met and eventually married my first wife. We were aged 21 and 20 respectfully when, after a seven-year courtship in which we had faced many family crises together, my fiancée and I decided to marry.

Linda and I had met as teenagers in Detroit Lakes, Minnesota a popular resort close to Winnipeg. She was working the summer as a nanny, and

I was vacationing with my family. A mutual friend, now a distinguished psychiatrist in Boston, introduced us. We dated off-and-on while both of us struggled to cope with family problems. Linda, for one thing, helped me to forget the emotional demands of my mother. In time we became the best of friends, intellectually compatible, with a similar vision and outlook on life. Following the wedding and a whirlwind honeymoon in New York City, we returned to Winnipeg where I completed my Master's Degree in Psychology and she obtained her Bachelor Degree in Education.

My marriage was a smooth, relatively tranquil period of my life in which I felt content with my role as husband, and family provider. Developing a career and establishing an identity in the community were at the roots of an extended period of happiness.

We lived a frugal life as students subsisting on money we received from our wedding guests. Many a time we had no money in the bank. Too proud to go to our parents for help we relied on friendly relatives who gave us a meal and a warm welcome. Later in life we would repay members of the family with our hospitality.

Those initial years were trying as the birth of Jason followed. There were many challenges, including my father's ill health and my mother's refusal to give up her emotional dependency on me. Caught between the needs of my biological family and my wife's needs we decided to move away from Winnipeg.

My acceptance as a PhD candidate in Clinical Psychology at the University of Ottawa afforded us the opportunity to pursue a life independent of family pressure. It was a new life and we did well. My wife enjoyed her work as a teacher-librarian eventually going back to get her Master's Degree in Library Science. I thrived in my new career as a psychologist.

We formed close and lasting friendships and supported each other in many ways as we welcomed three sons within five years.

No life is perfect and no marriage without trials and tribulations. Yet we had a loving and enduring relationship. Unexpectedly, life took a dramatic turn that shook the marriage to its foundation resulting in our not being able to survive together.

LIFE'S LESSON—*Two individuals do not a marriage make. Marriage is based on two individuals united and committed no matter what perils await them.*

CHAPTER 5

—◆—

INTO THE ABYSS

I often preach to my clients that living life well is relatively simple: know yourself, know your values, live by them. Yet I was about to break one of my basic values and in the process cause an upheaval that would fundamentally change the entire direction of my life.

The joy and challenge of being the new director of psychology was exhilarating. I was caught in a vortex of activity at best stimulating and at worst exhausting. Although the curve was steep, I soon learned that the world of hospital administration is highly competitive and political with each department vying for limited resources. It was like being in a gifted classroom trying to get the teacher's notice. In order to thrive in that atmosphere I realized early on that I needed to be seen as both competent and highly visible at the management board. I accomplished this by volunteering to serve on many hospital committees, including the informatics committee that was mandated to bring the latest technology to the hospital. My lack of knowledge of computers did not seem to matter in my selection to the committee.

To enhance the department's visibility I made myself available as a lecturer and consultant and on one occasion gave a presentation on stress to family practitioners. The lecture took place in a large amphitheatre with the lectern placed at the bottom facing a sea of faces focused on me. I felt like a gladiator being devoured by the lions. Despite perspiration obliterating my notes I successfully completed the lecture.

My work also involved training family therapists and I served with the marital and family therapy unit that dealt with the most difficult cases. The unit quickly developed a reputation as a highly competent and useful resource. Typically, the unit was composed of a psychologist, a psychiatrist, a social worker, a nurse and students from various disciplines. Other team members viewed interviews with a couple or with a family in a one-way mirror. Since I was the director I led case discussions that were frank, insightful and represented a welcome opportunity to learn from colleagues. On one occasion I was discussing a certain technique and no doubt felt empowered by my position. I claimed I had invented the technique but one of my students piped up: "You didn't invent that, it was a technique of Munichin."

My humbling mistake followed by the truth coming from a student during candid and disarming discussions was for me almost traumatic. Yet this would prove to be one of the most challenging and ultimately rewarding moments of my career.

An important member of the team was Dr. Barbara, a psychiatrist and a woman with short blond hair in her early forties who possessed an attractive hourglass figure that was neatly packaged in the most fashionable and professional business suit. Her presence on the team was to shatter my protected and sheltered life.

LIFE'S LESSON—*One must learn to cope with the roadblocks and detours that life brings. The closest line between two points is not always a straight line*

CHAPTER 6

THE DEEPER THE SORROW
THE MORE JOY YOU CAN CONTAIN

How, you might ask, does a seemingly normal, competent family man who _,by all objective criteria __appears on the surface to be a devoted husband and father become (if only briefly) one of "them"?

Yet there I was. A successful and professional clinical psychologist newly named as director of psychology at a major teaching hospital in Ottawa along with being the proud father of three active teenage sons and seemingly happily married for more than 20 years to a beautiful, warm and loving wife.

On the surface, my wife and I had it all. We maintained a close, intimate friendship and love that had stood the test of time. Together, we survived many crises and challenges; not the least of which was moving from our hometown of Winnipeg to Ottawa—where we knew no one—so that I could pursue my PhD. We were a good team, had met as teenagers, married young and devoted ourselves to our children and families.

In hindsight, after five years of individual psychotherapy and countless sleepless nights, I now have some insight into what *was* and what was to follow. They include painful personal events.

It seems my former wife and I had a co-dependency or enmeshed relationship in which we were dependent on each other in order to protect ourselves from the external world. Two parallel events occurred simultaneously between us that served to undermine the relationship.

My first wife (I have, as yet, no second wife) was becoming stronger and a more independent and complete person. At the same time I was undergoing a mid-life crisis in which I questioned everything including my identity, my values, my purpose in life. Given that I was unable to recognize my fears and anxieties or to express my needs directly we were a disaster waiting to happen. Nor were we able to find a safe harbour to wait out the storm.

I repeat that one member of the marital and family therapy unit was a female psychiatrist, Dr. Barbara. She was intelligent and compassionate and she played the role of mother to the unit while I took on the role of father.

At first, Dr. Barbara and I enjoyed a highly exciting and mutually respectful professional relationship. She was a skilled clinician and a gifted educator and we both enjoyed our teaching roles. As mother and father to the team we always demonstrated our professional competencies but were totally unaware of the undercurrent of sexual tension, attraction and bonding that was occurring. Doing co-therapy with Dr. Barbara was a magical and uplifting experience. We were dancers totally in sync with each other's moves, thoughts and emotions. It was as if I knew exactly what she would say and do before she actually did it. She, in turn, was totally aware of my interventions. Co-therapy was like giving a command performance before the Queen and being acknowledged by her for our special skills.

Unknown to me Dr. Barbara was experiencing a void in her marriage. We were like a dry and arid forest, taking only a tiny spark to ignite into an uncontrolled fire and passion that was impossible to extinguish. What followed were the most chaotic, dysfunctional and irresponsible days of my life.

Confused, uncertain and with no road map to follow, my life catapulted out of control. At times I felt euphoric and lived life for the moment. But that ecstasy was followed by intense guilt, shame and remorse. It was as if my rational logical side was moving in one direction while my emotional side was moving in the other. The subsequent devastation and destruction of the family I loved and cherished literally took away the only life I had known. I was left totally destroyed and in despair.

Over the course of my career, I have counselled literally thousands of men and women who have had an affair as a result of an unmet need in their primary relationship. I was now one of them. We were the unspoken cadre of men and women who have broken their vows, betrayed their partners and consequently been judged and condemned by society.

What followed was the most difficult six months of my life. How was I to live with the guilt, shame, fear, pain, sorrow and anxiety that I had caused those closest to me? I stopped talking to my wife. Suddenly the river between us was impossible to cross. In my desperation to alleviate my guilt, I confessed all, thereby exacerbating the pain and sorrow.

My world turned upside down. It was as if a cyclone had hit, leaving nothing in its wake but turmoil, death and destruction. All my family, particularly my wife and children, harshly condemned me as a selfish and evil man who had committed a carnal sin and therefore deserved absolutely no compassion or understanding. As a man who had lived his entire life caring for others, I was utterly lost.

Tremendous pain, both emotional and physical, saturated my being. I felt isolated and without identity or purpose. I managed to keep myself together during the day by becoming a workaholic. I was able to focus and concentrate on patient problems thereby forgetting or denying my own problems. Then, at night, I returned to the apartment. It was the apartment I had rented on a monthly basis in the foolish hope that I would be able to return to my home and former wife. It was not to be.

Having bought the entire contents of the apartment from the previous tenant, an American diplomat, I at least had a private place to mourn my losses. One of my most valued possessions in those early days was a beat-up bike that was included in the contents. Little did I know then that it would be my most important means of coping with my troubles.

After preparing my dinner—cold cuts, frozen TV dinners and the occasional pizza—I would eat alone then retire to bed where I would cry uncontrollably until I literally exhausted myself. My mind raced wondering how I could rectify the situation and reclaim my former life. I would ride that beat-up bike through the streets of Ottawa feeling strangely invisible as if I were observing other people live their lives. Yet I had no life. My body ached as if I had been horsewhipped. I felt extreme pain on the right side of my face that felt like pins entering me. I later learned I had a form of neuralgia that is a direct result of stress.

As I roamed aimlessly through the streets I questioned my entire life and whether it was worth going on.

I often forced myself to eat. It was a short-term solution. I was not at all certain there was going to be one in the long term.

On October 01, 1987, I started private practice with a total of $5,000 in my savings account. I had taken the precautionary measure of a six-month unpaid leave of absence from my position as director of psychology, but inwardly I knew I would not be returning.

The break-up of my family was to exact enormous financial pressures on me. It was like starting over again. I was determined that my family would not suffer any further by my mistakes and I made every effort to maintain their lifestyle.

Leaving the security of the public sector was probably a bad move on my part yet I had put in place a chain of events that I felt powerless to stop.

Then I got a desperately needed break. In that first week of private practice I signed a contract to be the employee assistance provider (EAP) in Ottawa for a major national organization. My financial concerns immediately diminished. I had been given a new lease on life.

As a person who valued structure, I now had none. I was still not convinced my marriage was irreparable. In an effort to reconcile I met weekly with my wife at my office. I tried to convince her to give me a second chance but she was too hurt and angry to consider reconciliation although I sensed she was uncertain about what to do. In desperation I sought the names of marital therapists from a colleague. We met in the waiting room, silently waiting for the therapist to call our names and relieve us of the tension and anger. The therapist tried to get us to talk it out but anger, hurt and sadness prevented real understanding. Finally, in a moment filled with extreme anger, I was told by my now ex-wife. "I can't do this anymore".

I left the therapist's office feeling pain and sadness that literally stopped me in my tracks. I did not know what to do, where to go, whom to call. I sat in my battered station wagon, crying uncontrollably like a baby searching for his mother. Life as I had known it was over.

LIFE'S LESSON—*Where there is an end there is a new beginning. Where there is despair there is hope for renewal and change.*

Chapter 7

The Beginning Of Healing—
Not To Have Pain Is Not To Be Human

As I oscillated between two different worlds, I could not find comfort neither in the world I had known nor the world I now occupied. I literally moved in and out of the family home while alternating between moods of depression and despair to dissatisfaction, restlessness and extreme tension. It was as if I had undermined all the sense of security and belonging I had known. I felt like a stranger in my own home.

This period of oscillation, restlessness, despair and enormous psychological pain was to last several months. It felt like forever. I was a lost soul drifting downstream toward the waterfall.

As a caring, compassionate, empathetic man whose entire life had been devoted to others I no longer had the capacity to care for myself. I knew I was in trouble. Though reluctant to share my private conflicts and transgressions I sought advice and counsel from two sources whom I highly valued—my clergy and a colleague. I approached them as a highly respected professional whose image was of a well-grounded man. Unknown to most, my inner world was filled with self-doubt and uncertainty.

"No man is an island," it is said but, unfortunately, when one plays the role of emotional healer it is difficult for others to provide support. Thus it came to be that I received emotional support from people whom I least expected it.

Early in the process, I was searching for a place to live. Unexpectedly, a colleague who had experienced a similar trauma many years previous, offered me a temporary sanctuary. I was deeply touched by his most generous and kind act. Similarly, others who had faced similar losses in their lives had a kind word or gesture that made all the difference in the world.

One night I was feeling particularly vulnerable, lonely and sad as I aimlessly walked the streets of Ottawa. It was as if I was in a sealed bubble, surrounded by people whom I could see but not touch. Arriving at my office late at night, a miracle suddenly happened. The noise of the phone pierced the silence of the night. Who would call me at this time? I t was Mo, a man who had been mentor and friend to me, whose outwardly sloppy and unkempt appearance, baggy pants hanging low with oversized, ill fitting cardigan sweaters which had seen better days, belied his razor sharp intellectual and emotional perceptions. Somehow, Mo, my surrogate father, had heard of my separation and had reached me to console me. It was the spark of light I needed to continue my journey of life.

Finally, deep into my despair, I did what I always tell my patients to do. I openly admitted to myself and later to others that I needed help.

I called my Rabbi, a kind, caring, and totally present gentleman, whom I expected would lecture me on my sins but instead gave me emotional support and—most importantly—did not criticize or judge my self-confessed inappropriate behaviour. This was to be the beginning of a long healing process.

Not only did the Rabbi offer me emotional support but also he proposed a way in which I could emerge from my cocoon to once again become an active member of my community. He offered to go running with me at the local community centre; a gesture that was deeply appreciated. The Rabbi would later prove a valuable friend when I went through the Get (a formal Jewish divorce before a rabbinical court) that was to prove emotionally draining and one of the lowest periods of my life.

In seeking professional assistance for myself I also turned to a friend and colleague by the name of Dr. Sam. When Dr. Sam realized my pain he gave me the names of five therapists whom he knew. I was familiar with four of them and chose the one I did not know. I had hesitated and debated with myself many days before I came to the conclusion that I had to take the therapy.

I can tell you that first call to Dr. Ann was filled with incredible anxiety and fear. Here I was the great emotional caretaker admitting I needed help. What a failure, what a fraud I was! I also felt useless and inadequate. It was as if I was nothing and had nothing to offer anyone.

My first appointment with Dr. Ann was filled with trepidation. Nevertheless, this very attractive Francophone with a strong connection to the Montreal Jewish community, proved over a five-year period to be a wonderful agent of change. As a practising psychoanalyst, Dr. Ann was sensitive enough not to insist I lie down on her couch, but instead honoured my request to engage in talk therapy, where I felt some degree of control. Although there were times when I questioned her therapy for the most part I came to understand my inner demons and what I needed to do to become whole again.

My process of healing took years; perhaps delayed by deep feelings of shame, guilt and the pain I had caused the people I loved most in my life. My healing continues to this day. I'm not sure I'll ever get over it but I have learned to cope and move on with my life.

If there is a lesson I learned it is the necessity to reach out to others for help and support. Life is full of constant surprises and, more often than not, those whom you expect to be there for you are not, and others quite unexpectedly provide you with the will and courage to face your demons.

One colleague, a woman born and raised in a small Ottawa Valley town who was there for me, was Ms. June, an attractive blonde or redhead. I'm never sure which. This was, Ms June, statuesque woman with deep penetrating blue eyes that instantly hold your focus and speak volumes of the kindness and compassion she exudes.

I first met her some thirty years ago after I won a competition to provide psychological services to unemployed clients of Employment and Immigration Canada and she became a lifelong friend.

I shall never forget my first experience with her as a consultant. After an hour's car ride into the Ottawa Valley, I anxiously entered the doorway of a large, imposing limestone building. I was not sure who I would see or what I was supposed to do.

Ms. June, a woman of enormous compassion, met me at the top of a long stairway with a warm, smile while all the time holding her infant son John. I was given a tour of the facilities and then ushered into a rather stark boardroom, complete with a modest looking oak table that had seen better days. A pleasant aroma filled the room. On the table were a coffee urn and a large assortment of doughnuts. As a teenager I had joined a social club simply because they served doughnuts at their meetings. I soon realized I had found my second home.

Ms. June's warmth and nurturing gestures were exactly what my broken soul needed. During many visits to this Ottawa Valley town, June and I formed both a professional and personal bond. First we devoted our energy to the clients but later conversation addressed personal concerns. We were kindred spirits who instantly understood each other and connected at a deep and meaningful level. As Ms. June liked to say: "Our lives touch lives."

Today, some 30 years later, I still refer to Ms. June as the best damn vocational counsellor in the country. And I am pleased to say Ms. June and I are still good friends and continue to collaborate professionally.

One of the major lessons I had to learn in order to heal myself was not to put all my eggs in one basket. As a married man my wife was my best friend, lover and confidante. Although we had many couples as friends most of my male friends were more people to do things with. Thus, if I wanted to go to a hockey game or play cards, I called these friends. In most cases to have a deep intimate conversation about one's emotional status was simply not on the cards.

Post divorce, although I still maintain contact with these friends, I have developed deep emotional friendships with other men and women from all walks of life.

LIFE'S LESSON—*Do not put all your eggs in one basket.*

CHAPTER 8

—◆—

SINGLE AGAIN

During the next year of my life destiny had me in a constant flux. Having changed job, family status, residence, friends and social status, there was one change I refused to make.

I was driving a grey, four-door station wagon that had seen better days. One particular problem, not a big deal in family life but a major concern in single life, was the passenger door on the right-hand front of the car would not open either from outside or inside. To get to the front seat, one had to enter via the driver's door and unceremoniously crawl over on all fours. To my teenage sons, this was not a problem but to a man going out on his first date in 20 years it would prove to be a major deterrent. To see the look of the tall, beautiful Susan, in short skirt trying to negotiate passage to her designated place—all the while trying to maintain dignity and self-respect—was to see someone shocked and bewildered. Susan fast dumped me as not cool enough. Like the cool dude in *My Cousin Vinny* I had my own acid test as to who for me was a keeper. Those women who coped with the car door problem proved to be women of substance.

After being out of the single market for more than 20 years, I naively entered the dating scene like a lamb to the slaughter. As a competent professional I sought the advice and counsel of others who had faced this daunting task. A woman close to me (you know who you are) told me: "*Don't* buy dinner on the first date, let them offer to pay. *Don't* be surprised if they open the door for you. *Don't,* whatever you do, talk about your ex. *Don't* tell them how much money you make. *Don't* sleep with them on the first date and when you do practise safe sex etc., etc.

You get the picture!

At first, when you become single again, your family and friends are anxious to fix you up. It's as if single men are going against all the rules of social engagement and are considered incomplete or, far worse, not a real member of society unless coupled. In many ways dating, as a mature adult (whatever that means), is analogous to being a teenager again only with more angst, self-doubts and anxiety. In summary it is awkward in conversation about what to do, where to go and when. So many questions, so few answers!

At first, I tried too hard and asked too many questions in a poor attempt to cover my anxiety thereby scaring anyone who might have been interested in me. Later, as I became more confident, eye contact and other non-verbal cues allowed a higher degree of success.

Mature women have literally changed the social mating game. Women of today have all kinds of resources at their disposal and know exactly what they want, do not want and how to get what they want. Single naive men stand no chance at all.

One such encounter will give you insight into the modern day world of dating. I first met Betty as a result of an advertisement she placed in a community paper. She was trying to attract single people to a golf tournament. After reading her ad, I phoned and talked with her on the phone and suggested we meet before the event. We decided to play golf, an opportunity to spend five hours together in a relaxed environment. In summary I met a beautiful blonde knockout with an hourglass figure and dazzling personality. She exuded class and social flair. I was no match for this dynamic bombshell.

I tried to engage her with my wit and physical attributes. Unfortunately, she was a serious student of the game and did not need my assistance on the golf course. A whirlwind romance followed a most enjoyable game of golf and a satisfying dinner. I was utterly mesmerized by her beauty and felt like putty in her hands. Fortunately for me Betty was also an empathetic, caring and sensitive woman who realized my emotional vulnerability and in many ways helped me to re-enter the adult world. For that, I will always remain eternally grateful to her.

These were heady times for me, analogous to being in the candy store and allowed the choice of any candy my heart desired. I was astonished that mature women were attracted to me. It seemed women were attracted to professional, articulate and sensitive men and not shy about stating their intentions and desires.

I found the dating game exciting and highly stimulating. However, it soon proved tiring. It seems most of us singles seek a long term, committed relationship.

Single life fell into the pattern of working, looking after the children during the week they lived with me and trying to have some sort of social life. I experienced great joy in co-parenting my children with life oscillating each week from having all the responsibility to having none. After a second change in family circumstances, when my ex found a new partner, the boys decided to live with me full time. I had been given a second chance and I was determined to make things right.

LIFE'S LESSON—*Life always allows opportunities to learn from one's mistakes and to get it right.*

CHAPTER 9

MY THREE SONS

Parenting meant sacrifices, postponing needs and in my case also being there for my three teenage sons. This was a role I would thrive on. This was an opportunity as a natural caretaker to develop my relationship with my boys. Although I have been accused of having a *laissez-faire* style of parenting, for the most part I believe I taught my three sons sound values.

I will attempt to give you a glimpse into this very special time of my life. In order to make my life easier, I made arrangements for the boys to have a small, four-wheel drive Jeep. As any family of teenagers eligible to drive knows, the family car tends to be the focus of intense discussions. In part, the Jeep enabled me to have access to my own car, but I recall many occasions when I took the bus to work.

Anyway Daniel, all of sixteen years old at the time, drives the Jeep onto the driveway and for reasons that will become apparent, takes a cloth and covers the rear licence plate. No words are exchanged between us but he seems a little quiet and downtrodden. Soon after, the doorbell rings and a female police officer asks if she can come in to talk to me. I let her in. She proceeds to tell me this incredible story of how my youngest son is reputed to have passed a school bus when it was stopped to let children off. Apparently this happened a short time ago and was reported to the police by the school bus driver. The police officer wanted to lay a charge under the *Highway Traffic Act*. Playing the single parent card, I tried to persuade the officer there was a misunderstanding and that Daniel had learned his lesson. Couldn`t she let him off with a warning? She issued a ticket and left.

Daniel and I talked. I took a soft, understanding approach. Apparently, he passed the school bus driver because he believed the driver waved him on. I believed him.

What followed was a demonstration that I was there for him. We hired a lawyer, a Queen`s Counsel no less. Coming from a family of distinguished lawyers, I was aware of the demands of the court to provide credible evidence. We took photos of the roadway attempting to show there was no way it could have occurred the way the school bus driver told it. In addition, our lawyer attempted to plea bargain with the Crown Counsel, but it was to no avail as there is no lesser charge under the *Highway Traffic Act.*

Finally, it was the big day. We had hoped that either the school bus driver or the officer would not show. They showed up. Sitting nervously in court awaiting our hearing the situation looked bad for us when the judge fined a young man for being disorderly in public after earlier in the day he had been released from a psychiatric facility.

Our case was called. Daniel testified and frankly gave a marvellous account. I was a proud father. The school bus driver gave dramatically different evidence. Despite our best efforts it was a question of believing an adult or a teenager. It was no contest. We were found guilty and ordered to pay a huge fine. I walked out of the courtroom with my arm around my son. He learned a hard lesson that life is not fair at times. Nevertheless, it was an experience I cherish because I know my son knows how much he is loved and supported by me. I am confident now that he is a father that he in turn will be there for his children.

Similarly, one evening as I was preparing to go out on a date to celebrate my birthday, I heard a soft whimpering from Greg`s door. I knocked and asked permission to enter. I could tell that my son was very upset about something. He knew I was going out on a date but I immediately recognized that he needed me more at that instance than my need to celebrate. We talked for an hour and then hugged.

One of the benefits of being a single parent is the opportunity to travel independently with your children. I have been blessed to travel to the Middle East, South Africa and Europe with them. But the story I will tell here involves travel closer to home. One Christmas season, we decided to go to Myrtle Beach, North Carolina, the undisputed golfing capital of the world. Travelling by car, an 18-hour trip, afforded me a rare opportunity to interact with my three sons as a family unit.

Shortly after leaving Ottawa, Daniel—then all of 12 years of age—piped out: "This trip is going to be a male bonding experience." Indeed it was.

A conversation ensued about safe sex. Before I could offer a single word, Daniel gave a perfect explanation as to what was what. Today, the fact that I am the proud grandfather of five grandchildren I attribute in part to my failure to tell the boys about birth control.

That trip to Myrtle Beach was a blast, not only for the golf and the experience of playing at a PGA-rated course on Christmas day for absolutely no charge because we were fortunate enough to overhear a local talk about it but more importantly for the quality time spent getting to know each other.

I always knew my children's needs were important and, with the exception of a brief time in my life when I was so filled with shame and despair that I could not take care of myself let alone three teenagers, I treated them that way. I believe they know how much I love them and will always be there for them.

Being a single parent has its trials and tribulations. There are times when one must be firm. Disagreement does happen. However, respect for each other, solid values, good communication and an understanding of each other's needs go a long way to a foundation of trust and love.

LIFE'S LESSON—*Being a loving family unit can take on more different forms than a traditional nuclear family.*

CHAPTER 10

A NEW SOCIAL REALITY

What I found terrifying was how to fill the void after the dissolution of my marriage. Suddenly I did not have a partner to make social arrangements. So I had a choice to sit home alone between four walls feeling sorry for myself or to make arrangements myself.

At first, I attended singles events like dinners, wine-tasting, etc. I would frequently go alone and was assigned (if lucky) to an age-related table where one could strike up an interesting conversation. One was forced to rely on long-forgotten social skills to survive. Despite my personal challenge of conversing with a minimum of three people at any social event I attended, I often left feeling alone and dejected.

Soon after my separation I was invited to a singles event in which four men and four women met for a potluck dinner. These types of dinners can be a non-threatening way of meeting like-minded people. At that time my baby sister was also single and a veteran and *maven* (an expert who knows all) of the single scene. Despite scepticism we entered the host home energized and prepared to contribute to the evening. Little did I know we would be the entertainment!

At first, both my sister and I tried with little success to engage the others in social conversation. People ate silently, almost passively, telling us to be quiet. After a concerted effort on my part, I simply gave up and left my sister to continue her monologue. Both of us left disappointed and discouraged with the single life.

Luckily, on other occasions, I was fortunate enough to meet dynamic and enlightened people. I dated several intelligent, attractive professional women who seemed to be leading interesting lives. One most valuable lesson I learned from these women was to be open to life's experiences.

One of the mainstays of the single community is the weekend dance, usually held at a large impersonal freezing hockey rink or church hall. Dances for single people are an opportunity to meet others and let off steam. More often than not the music is the rock'n roll we danced to as teenagers. I recall the absolute fear and trepidation I felt when I first entered those halls. Asking a strange woman to dance was more difficult for me than speaking to a thousand people. However, like all skills, if you persevere you soon become more comfortable.

I recall arriving at one dance with my buddy, fast Eddie, a short, highly energetic man who had no fear or inhibition. Upon entering Eddie spotted two gorgeous women. Eddie shouted to me: "You take the tall one and I'll take the short one." What followed was a whirlwind romance of intrigue and an accelerated course in the life of single people. I confess that after that experience I was no longer a rookie in the dating game.

One of the major tenets I learned is that men don't get it. By that I mean women are much better at bonding and providing emotional support for each other.

Like most men of my generation I put all my eggs in one basket. My ex-wife was my only friend, confidante and lover. So, when circumstances drove us apart, I was left without an adequate social support system. As a single man I tried to rectify that situation. Forming bonds with other men is extremely difficult. Most men were either emotionally incapable or simply not interested. I believe it is the reason most single men do not cope well with single life and thus often reattach for the wrong reasons. Men need to learn to express their emotions, to value friendships and have a better balance in their lives. At a time of emotional crisis, the job or the Blackberry is no substitute for a good friend.

I am blessed with several close male friends today, offering each other a much-needed support system. A female patient described her trio of supporters as her board of directors. When confused and uncertain she relied on her board to reflect and offer her advice and guidance.

LIFE'S LESSON—*We men would do well to emulate women's strong social support network.*

CHAPTER 11

IT'S OVER!

A time of intense emotional pain, despair and a feeling of being rudderless had followed my separation. I felt like a cloud floating through the sky at the mercy of winds of change.

Not knowing who, what and where I was, I clumsily tried to navigate my way out of my messed-up life. I refused to give up on my previous life and made repeated attempts at reconciliation, all of which failed. That further undermined my already battered self-image. It would take the reappearance of all four seasons before I began to accept that my marriage was really over.

The event that sealed my fate occurred on a typical Ottawa winter afternoon when I was enjoying the company of my children. The phone rang ominously, interrupting the laughter and a close family moment. It was a friend who blurted out rather insensitively to me: "David, did you realize your ex-wife got married yesterday?" I dropped the phone shocked, speechless and utterly in disbelief. It felt like the time many years ago when my brother hit me in the face when we were boxing and I fell to the ground gasping for air. After what seemed like an hour but probably was minutes, I told my friend I would get back to him. I immediately asked my children about their mother's new marital status and they confirmed that indeed it was true and rather nonchalantly continued what they were doing. I was out of the loop and left to my own to find a way to cope with this devastating news. There was no turning back the clock. I was now truly flying solo.

I felt rejected and isolated by this final kick in the chain of events. Despite my despair, I was able to function effectively as a psychologist and turned my attention to my work and to the challenge of becoming a father with shared custody. I renewed my efforts and literally doubled my clientele in order to fill the void in my life. Working meant I did not have to concentrate on solving the myriad of problems I had created and was a most acceptable way to avoid making the difficult decisions I needed to address to move on. Having suffered a financial setback and being a workaholic had the dual advantage of my making a lot of money as well as offering a quick way to repair my battered self-image. In many respects my personal woes made me a more caring and compassionate person and ultimately a better psychologist.

What about my role as a father to three active teenage sons? To say my indiscretion played havoc with my relationship with my children is only to touch the surface of the pain, anger and uncertainty it caused. As a man totally involved in raising his children, I was aware that my indiscretion severely damaged my relationship with them. No longer was I a role model and a man of integrity with whom they could share their most intimate secrets. Instead, I became a source of anger, frustration and a total enigma to them.

They had no idea who this man was who had biologically sired them. Unknown to them, I too had no idea of the person I had become. Given this uncertainty, confusion, chaos and a restructured family, I set out to be the father I wanted to be and to rebuild the trust and confidence of my children. It would take many years to accomplish that task. I believe for the most part I succeeded.

Needing a place to live in large enough to house my three sons and me proved a difficult undertaking. My first success involved renting a fully furnished, two-bedroom condo from an elderly Jewish woman who was going south for the winter. It was a win-win situation. She found a reliable Jewish doctor who would respect her possessions and I found a comfortable safe environment to provide shelter for my family and me.

Mrs. B was gregarious and warm and she welcomed me to her condo like a long lost relative. Smelling the sweet aroma of fresh-baked moon cookies reminded me of my youth when a great aunt from Russia would bake them for my brother and me. Similarly, her furniture was of a heavy texture with vivid lime and orange colours. At the time I chose this condo, I did not fully realize that at some unconscious level I was looking for my childhood home where I would feel safe to begin the long healing process.

I eventually moved into a large two-bedroom apartment that allowed me to provide for my children's needs. At first, I felt helpless and inept with domestic responsibilities. Cooking, cleaning, laundry and other domestic chores, once the domain of my ex-wife, became activities to master for survival. Not unexpectedly any new skill at first usually appeared daunting, but with perseverance and a willingness to practise and learn, mastery or at least competency arrived. One such skill for survival was cooking. To eat is to live. Although initially we ate out constantly the novelty soon wore off. The children were begging for a home-cooked meal.

Having obtained a PhD, like all good academics, I realized that to master a new skill it is advisable to consult others with know-how. So I obtained recipes, cookbooks and family secrets that somehow had provided kitchen skills for past generations of my family. If it was good enough for them it was good enough for my children. I tried to please my children by following the advice of a close family member who gave me the recipe for a spaghetti sauce that turned into a six-hour cooking odyssey. I cut, boiled and re-cut the various ingredients for this tomato-based sauce.

After proudly serving my very first meal to my children, I awaited the verdict. Jason reacted with the question: "What is this shit?"

After my teary-eyed breakdown an order for pizza restored order.

Nevertheless, with determination and stubbornness, I was able to master the art of putting a wholesome, home-cooked meal on the table for my children. Indeed, on one occasion when my brother was visiting, I served him a fine meal of broiled salmon, fried rice and salad that absolutely amazed him. His remark to me was: "You'd make someone a good wife." What he had noticed was that I was now a complete person equally in touch with feminine and masculine sides. I was ready to enter into a wholesome and life sustaining relationship.

LIFE'S LESSON—*What at first seems a hardship can turn into a challenge and an opportunity for strong personal growth.*

CHAPTER 12

Wow!

Suddenly and most unexpectedly, it happened!

After my divorce, I met numerous attractive women with whom I could connect on several levels but I never felt that any of them was my *besercht*, my true soul mate. Orthodox Jews believe that 40 days before your birth you meet your soul mate. The belief is that 40 days before your birth it is pre-determined who is the one who will complete your soul. For reasons I am not entirely aware of, I always found fault with any suitable partner. They were not warm enough, too critical, too material, and too religious. You get the picture.

One weekend, I attended a Jewish singles convention sponsored by the local Jewish community centre involving singles from all walks of life congregating to worship, socialize and meet each other with the hope they would find their *besercht*. On this one particular Friday (Shabbat in the Jewish religion), I attended the opening cocktail party and was set on working the room, making small talk with people I knew or was meeting for the first time. Suddenly, there was my princess! A woman of breathtaking beauty, long dark flowing hair, soft translucent skin, perfect white teeth and a tall, supple body of perfect proportion. She left me breathless, speechless and immobilized.

As the audience took their seats for the magic show, would you believe it, my princess volunteered to assist the magician. Not one male in the audience saw or cared about the show!

Afterwards, I screwed up my courage, nervously approached the princess and initiated a conversation with her. Truth be told, she was as nice and kind as I had imagined. After driving her home to her brother we arranged to meet at the dance the next evening.

I arrived at the dance "dolled up" in my finest suit only to find my princess cavorting with a tall, handsome man who clearly had her fancy. She totally ignored my attempt to engage her. Devastated, rejected and unprepared for defeat, I attempted to make the best of a bad situation. I tried to socialize with others but my heart was not in it. I left deeply disappointed and sad. This feeling would revisit me time and time again with thoughts of my princess.

However, I am a man who was raised to believe in himself. If you really want something, my father always said, go and get it. Persistence, stubbornness and tenacity are traits that have served me well. On that first evening I met my princess I was astute enough to have obtained her home telephone number.

Thus begins my campaign to woe her. I attempted to keep it light. My calls were always upbeat and affirming. A major obstacle to the process was the fact the princess lived in Montreal, a two-hour drive from Ottawa.

Over several months, my princess politely rebuffed any possible contact and offered excuse after excuse not to meet me. Nevertheless, I was a man possessed. Finally, after literally months of telephone contact, my princess agreed to meet me for coffee. Excitement and pure joy ruled supreme as I literally flew down the highway to our designated rendezvous. I was finally with my princess who had treated me with a certain aloofness that only served to whet my appetite. Being polite, we talked but did not connect in any meaningful way. I left once again disappointed.

Several months passed and for reasons I cannot articulate, I felt an unexplained urge to call her. Timing and opportunity are everything in life. My princess had just completed a major renovation of her home that had totally pre-occupied her. She now seemed more open to meeting again,

We instantly connected this time on an emotional, physical and spiritual level. Unconsciously, as I played with her hair, we both felt a powerful and jolting inner spark that was purely magical. It was as if a strong outside force was pushing us toward each other.

Afterwards, she told me that she had fond memories of her grandfather lovingly touching her hair as a child. We talked and then talked some more, totally losing track of time. We were in our own space and completely unaware of others. It was as if we had known each other all of our lives. There was a sense of familiarity, despite our different paths that, perhaps in another life, we had known each other.

I arranged to take my princess out for her birthday the next week and the process of coupling began in earnest. Here were two people who, despite all odds, had truly found their soul mates, best friends and lovers.

What followed was a modern day love story that was not designed to be easy.

At first, I travelled to Montreal every weekend and, by honouring her need for privacy, I made arrangements to stay at friends or in hotels. All of you that are familiar with the dance of love are also acquainted with that light-headed sense of euphoria and energy that colours the perception of one in love. I was overjoyed that finally I had found true love and that the pain, suffering and sacrifices I had previously made were not in vain.

But after several months, I began to resent the expense and effort I was making to sustain the relationship. It felt one-sided. We began to argue about living arrangements and her need to protect her family. Her teenage children began to resent my presence in the family home. They were not prepared to have another male in their life.

I was deeply hurt that my concerns were not being heard. In retrospect, I was not sensitive enough to the children's pain and loss of their family unit. My princess took a passive and non-directive role in the proceedings. I felt that our relationship was not important enough for her to say something to her children. After three years together we were at an impasse. She wanted more space. I wanted more integration. Psychologist Bruno Bettelheim says love is not enough. Not surprisingly the relationship ended when we could not find a way to overcome our differences.

Once again I felt totally lost, sad and in despair at having lost the woman whom I truly loved. My mourning would be long, extensive and painful. In many ways, I felt worse than my marital break-up. My hopes and dreams were once again totally broken.

"People come into your life for a reason, a season or a lifetime and often it is never clear as to which category they belong. My princess and I have now parted ways and like any transitory relationship it is important to learn from it.

When someone is in your life for a reason it is usually to meet a need. You have expressed the feeling that they have come to assist you through a difficulty, to provide you with guidance and support, to aid you physically, emotionally or spiritually. They may seem like a g-d-send and probably are. They are there for the reason you need them to be there. Then, without any wrongdoing on your part or at an inconvenient time, this person will say or do something to bring the relationship to an end.

Sometimes they die and sometime they walk away. Sometimes they act up and force you to take a stand. What we must realize is that our need has been met, our desire fulfilled and that their work is done. The prayer you sent up has been answered and now it is time to move on.

Some people come into your life for a season, because your turn has come to share, grow or learn. They bring you an experience of peace and may make you laugh. They may teach you something you have never done. They usually give you an unbelievable amount of joy. Believe it. It is real for only a season. Lifetime relationships teach you lifetime lessons. They are things you must build upon to have a solid foundation.

Your job is to accept the lesson, love the person and put what you have learned to use in other relationships and areas of your life. It is said love is blind but friendship is clairvoyant."

LIFE'S LESSON—*People come into your life for a reason, a season or a lifetime. When you know which one it is, you will know what to do for that person*

CHAPTER 13

———◆———

WITH ARNIE IN ITALY

Following the dissolution of my marriage, I sought ways to regain some sort of social life that previously was the domain of my ex-wife. I also realized that I was now my own social secretary and if I didn't make plans nothing would happen. This was also the opportunity to try different activities.

I had always wanted to play the guitar. Who, of my generation, didn't want to emulate the great Elvis Presley? My desire to play was partially attributed to an event that occurred when I was a student in Grade 4 at Inkster Public School in Winnipeg, where all members of the class were required to be members of the choir. While skill level differed from one student to another, just where I stood on the skill ladder was made very clear to me when I was told by the choir director that it would be better if I silently mouthed the words rather than sang aloud.

I am convinced this slight directly contributed to my being a psychologist and years later attempting to learn the guitar. Details of my failed attempt are available to a chosen few. However, for the purposes of this manuscript, it is suffice to say that enthusiasm will only take you so far in learning a new skill.

Thus one crisp and frosty morning I was enjoying my daily coffee with another treat, Canada's national liberal newspaper *The Globe and Mail.* I was really looking for ways to enrich my life. Reading the personal ads, I came upon one that stated: *"Retired History Professor leads two-week tours of Europe. For mature adults."* Thinking of myself as reasonably mature, I immediately phoned to inquire. A very pleasant woman informed me that Professor Arnie was in Florida but would call me back the following week. Exactly as promised, I received the call from a gentleman who was to impress me as a warm, funny and energetic man. I felt an immediate kinship with him as we played Jewish geography (a who-do-you-know-where). I raised my concerns about the ages of the participants, but Arnie reassured me there would be some young ones.

I explored other travel options and reviewed the website describing in considerable detail the sites and sounds we were to visit in Italy. After a time of reflection I decided to take the two-week trip with Arnie. The sound of Paris, Nice, Sienna, Florence, Venice and Rome was that of far away exotic places intended for the rich and famous. I would soon be travelling among them.

Three months later, in the middle of May, I found myself walking through the vast corridors of Pierre Trudeau International Airport in Montreal looking for the Air France flight to Paris and my fellow travellers. At first, I didn't believe what my eyes beheld: an odd assortment of elderly men and women all decked out in the latest travel wear, co-ordinated from head to toe, each holding the same guidebook given to me by Arnie. These would be my travel companions for the next two weeks.

Surrounded by my fellow travellers was a slightly portly, bald-headed man with spectacles who looked very much like everyone's favourite teacher. Arnie was holding court with all around focused on his stories and jokes. Face-to-face with our fearless leader Professor Arnie, I was introduced and given the names of my travel companions. Taken aside, I was told clearly that the young ones would be meeting us in Paris.

After a pleasant flight to Paris the youngsters, aged in their 50s, embarked from their flight and I was pleasantly surprised to meet them. They were bright, attractive, fun-loving and highly energetic people. I knew then that this trip was going to be memorable. Despite the age differences, this happy band of 36 seniors managed to form a powerful and highly cohesive group. It was as if we all had decided to take care of each other. Thus, there was an endless supply of food, drinks, candies and any medication known to mankind that all were willing to share. It felt like summer camp on wheels.

One of the highlights of each day's activities was Arnie's joke of the day. Often off-colour and raunchy, it served to bind the group together. Arnie, a retired history professor, TV producer and prolific writer, would fill us with facts in stories of the Italian Renaissance, famous artists and other historical figures that would provide a wonderful setting to the amazing sites we saw. Arnie was the author of numerous novels and stage plays and the producer and judge of a longstanding quiz show for high school students, *Reach For The Top*. One example of Arnie's infectious personality and sense of humour occurred while we were on a highway in rural Italy. Looking off into the horizon, we saw what seemed like a white mountain. Arnie, in his most authoritative voice, remarked: "Look, snow!" Upon further inspection we realized we were seeing the beautiful famous white marble of Karenna.

This particular trip, one of many I took with Arnie, was especially enjoyable for me, as I had arranged to meet my eldest son, then twenty-three years of age and living in Israel, in Rome. Upon arrival, I entered my room and whom do you think I found sound asleep on my bed but Jason?

Jason travelled with our group to Rome, Sienna, Florence and Venice. Being everyone's grandson on the bus was a wonderful experience for him. However, I noticed at times he needed his own space and often he simply wandered away to explore the sites on his own.

Many of these seniors were simply amazing people never giving in to their frailties or infirmities. Their attitude toward life was a wonderful lesson for my son. They demonstrated time after time a sense of determination and grit coping with the grinds of international travel that would have exhausted a much younger group.

Thus began my international travel to more than 20 countries in Europe, Asia and Africa. Among the many countries I have seen by far the most interesting have been China, South Africa and Israel. To give a feel for how these travels have impacted me I have enclosed an article I wrote on China while serving on the editorial board of a community paper in Ottawa.

IMPRESSIONS OF CHINA, AUG. 4, 2006

Recently, I had the privilege to travel to China. China 2006 is becoming a major economic power and is enjoying unparalleled economic growth and development.

China is no longer the world of Confucius where respect, selflessness, obedience and a sense of community prevail. Indeed the values of old China can be found only in isolated segments of the population. The new China is dominated by commerce and capitalism.

According to Ted Fishman, author of CHINA INC., an award-winning analysis of China, the following facts are known:

- *3 million rural Chinese will move to cities in the next 15 years.*
- *China has more than 150 cities with a population greater than 1 million.*
- *China has 1.3 billion people—over one-fifth of the world's population.*
- *Apparel workers in China make $30 per week.*
- *Some 74 million Chinese families can now afford to buy cars.*
- *Currently in Beijing, in preparation for the 2008 Olympics, 2,000 high-rise buildings are underway.*

Having stated the facts, what is the effect of this massive change upon the Chinese people?

Depending if you are old or young, educated or not, live in an urban setting or not, your lot in this new Chinese society varies. Generally speaking, if you are a young, educated, urbanite, you probably enjoy a lifestyle that is fast approaching western standards with one noticeable exception. China's notorious one-child policy has resulted in a surplus of men (ratio 2:1) who cannot find suitable female partners. Women of marrying age are now in a position to demand the three Cs (cash, condo and car) before considering any serious marriage proposal.

I was told by my guide in Xian, the ancient capital of China, that her parents, who are over the age of 50, enjoy a small state pension and medical care whereby the young must pay for private insurance to cover their medical and hospital expenses.

The peasants, migrant workers and the disabled, who cannot afford insurance, go without medical treatment unless they are eligible for the special free medical check-ups provided during Handicap Week.

Throughout my travels in China, I was struck by the warmth, openness and generosity of the Chinese people. On arrival in Beijing, unable to sleep because of the time change, I wandered out of my hotel room to a nearby park where I found elderly men doing Tai Chi and more than happy to have me observe and photograph their private moments. A warm wave indicating that at some level we had connected.

Similarly, in Shanghai, a city of 17 million people, I was asked to take a family photo, only to be invited to be a part of the photo. A hardy handshake demonstrated once again mutual respect.

I saw seniors dancing and singing with a passion and a sense of community seldom seen in western society.

LIFE'S LESSONS

Despite these wonderful images of old China, China today is a country with many issues to resolve. An agrarian society, problems of poverty, homelessness, poor air quality and overcrowding now face the Chinese government. For reasons I do not fully comprehend, the Chinese have no patience for queuing in an orderly manner.

In Shanghai, I spent a delightful early morning watching from my 30th floor hotel room pedestrians literally dart through traffic. I watched with amazement at how trucks, cars and buses zigzagged to avoid pedestrians darting out at random.

I was told that any pedestrian who gets hit receives a life-long pension from the owner of the vehicle, thus explaining the skill and patience of the vehicle drivers.

Perhaps the most disheartening aspect of Chinese society I observed was the handicapped, the infirm and the disabled.

Although it is my understanding that the government has made efforts to deal with the issue, we saw beggars, grossly deformed children and adults of all ages resorting to begging and asking for handouts to survive. Everywhere foreign tourists went we had to run the gauntlet of these most desperate people.

China is fast becoming a major economic force, but its leaders need to remember their traditional values and find a way to honour and respect those members of the Chinese society who have not directly benefited from the pursuit of economic growth.

Until such time as all of her citizens are taken care of, China will not have truly joined the league of developed nations.

Although I have been fortunate to see the world it didn't exactly start out that way. To say I was a white-knuckle flyer gives you just a little hint of the anxiety and absolute terror I felt when flying. I tried everything to overcome my fear, including cognitive behaviour therapy, tranquillizers and taking courses on aviation. My most heartfelt apologies go to those unfortunate innocent passengers with whom to distract myself I tried non-stop talk.

One incident illustrates the extent of my fear of flying. I was scheduled to fly to France to participate in a biking tour of the Pyrenees. Mirabel Airport, the Canadian federal government's white elephant concession to Quebec, was then the departure point for international flights from Montreal. A close friend graciously agreed to drive me there. After being dropped off, I registered for my flight to Paris and waited for its boarding and departure. Looking at the dark and menacing sky, I worked myself

47

into a full-blown anxiety attack with the accompanying sweats, shaky hands and rapid heartbeat. Internally, I was seriously debating whether or not to get on that flight. Finally I chose not to go. By then I had to deal with the authorities. They surprisingly understood_ this was before the 9/11 events that changed the way the world works_and duly took my luggage off the plane.

Returning to Ottawa by bus, I tried to figure out how to deal with the inevitable embarrassment, the guilt, and what to say to friends and family. You can only imagine the kind of reception I received upon return to work. I was always subject to endless teasing by my friends and family regarding my fear of flying. Perhaps the most interesting reaction was my host in France when I arrived one year later. Chris's response was: "We've been waiting for you. What kept you?"

How did I overcome my fear of flying? Essentially, it really is mind over matter. I soon realized that my anxiety, like all anxiety, is fear of the unknown and fear of loss of control. I eventually reached a certain stage in my life when I simply realized we have very little control of our lives and to enjoy life one must learn to go with the flow.

Whether you believe in a higher power, the law of nature or serendipity, life happens when we least expect it. The only control we all have when flying is when we make our decision whether to get on the plane or not. Having counselled many pilots, I can assure you that they too want to live.

Thus I made my decision to fly simply because I was unwilling to give up the pleasure of seeing my grandchildren who live thousands of miles away on a regular basis, to stroll on a beach on the Indian Ocean, or, walk with my son up and down the hallowed and historic fairways of St. Andrew's golf course in Scotland, the birthplace of golf.

LIFE'S LESSON—*Each of us lives in a box. What differentiates one person from another is the size of the box they live in. Each of us must take personal responsibility for the size of the box we decide to live in. I have lived in a small confining box. Today, my box is the world and I rejoice in discovering its pleasures.*

Dad Mom
1940 Beausejour, Manitoba

Nozick family at home
419 McAdam Ave
Winnipeg, Manitoba 1953

David (age) 8 Stanley (age) 10
dressed as twins in our yard
Winnipeg, Manitoba 1953

David (age) 10 Jo-Anne (age) 2 Stanley (age) 12
419 McAdam Ave
Winnipeg, Manitoba 1955

Daniel (age) 18, 1993 in his room on Kibbutz Urim, Israel

David, Jason while on Arnie's Trip to Italy. 1993

David and Greg on Hogan's bridge.
18th hole, The Old Course
St. Andrew Links. St. Andrew, Scotland

Jason, David, Greg, Alfred while on safari
Kruger National Park, South Africa

David at Tiananmen Square
Beijing China

CHAPTER 14

$\longrightarrow$ ◆ $\longleftarrow$

TRAVELS WITH FAMILY

Having conquered my fear of flying I was ready to see the world. My children, world travelers all, have taken me to places I would not normally visit. Jason and Nicole have developed a wonderful tradition of taking extended parental leave after the birth of each child to travel to far and exotic places. I'm truly amazed how they do this with three children under the age of five.

Thus, one cold, clear day in January, I suddenly found myself on a KLM airline bus headed to Montreal's Trudeau International Airport to fly to Amsterdam to rendezvous with Greg and then meet up with Jason in Johannesburg, South Africa, the country of his wife's childhood. On the bus I noticed a refined, immaculately dressed elderly woman who was traveling alone. Engaging her in a conversation I soon learned she was also going to South Africa to visit her children and grandchildren.

On arrival in Montreal I proceeded to check in, pass security without incident and finally find a seat near the gate of the KLM flight. As we were ushered onto the plane a steward came on the intercom and announced that the original plane had had mechanical troubles and that we were waiting for a certified pilot to arrive from New York to fly the plane.

After a 90-minute wait the pilot arrived to a warm welcome. As I sat patiently in my customary aisle seat a steward asked if I might move to a middle seat to accommodate a family traveling with twin babies. I immediately thought of my own son's young family and did as requested ignoring the fact I had 18 hours of flight ahead of me that night.

After reaching cruising speed the steward ask me to come with him to the back of the 747-400. He ushered me to a single seat with a curtain surrounding me. It was my own private room. Before leaving me he opened a door at the rear of the plane and there before me was a large cargo space which he said could carry a live animal such as a rhinoceros. Wow! Soon I was fast asleep as we crossed the Atlantic Ocean.

Upon arrival at Schofeld airport in Amsterdam I left the plane quickly to catch my departure plane to Johannesburg and was pleasantly surprised at the efficiency of the Dutch. The departure gate was two minutes away. I had lots of time to explore and find the deli store and buy my friend the truffles I had promised.

Suddenly I saw Greg hurrying to our departure gate. A joyous reunion, an update on his travels in Europe and we were soon on the plane with 11 hours flying time to Johannesburg ahead. Somehow, charm runs thick in the Nozick clan. Greg managed to procure me a comfortable aisle seat while he had three seats to himself allowing him to sleep all the way to Joburg.

On arrival, Jason found us after debarking from his flight from Cape Town. After a short cab ride to the hotel and something to eat, it was early to bed as we had an adventuresome day ahead. My children, aware of their father's wanderings, and the crime-infested streets of Joburg, absolutely forbade me to leave the armed guarded hotel compound. I did as I was told for once.

After a very early morning wake-up call and a quick breakfast we were picked up by our pre-arranged van taking us to the world famous Kruger National Park, six hours north. Our fellow passengers included a German honeymoon couple and a recently retired couple from Australia. The highlight of the trip was the guide's monologue as we drove through the most incredible mountainous countryside. Our guide, a native white South African, informed us of the considerable challenges of living in this new majority-ruled and independent country.

We were glad to be out of the van on finally arriving at our rendezvous. Left alone we surveyed our surroundings taking in several open-air cafes, a couple of tourist shops with few tourists and mostly black service people. The air was hot and heavy.

Suddenly we were meet by this big exuberant black man wearing the uniform of the touring group we had hired. This was Alfred, our safari guide for the next three days. A loving, compassionate family man, Alfred was an ordained Lutheran minister and a man who took great pride in showing his park to the outside world. It soon became apparent that

Alfred knew every living species like the back of his hand. We were in good hands.

The unofficial mayor of Hazy view, the gateway to Kruger National Park, Alfred was eager to show us his domain. He shepherded us into an open safari jeep that was to be our second home for the next three days. The elevated jeep afforded us a panoramic view of our surroundings. It was designed to carry 12 passengers. The boys and I were to have exclusive use of the jeep for the next three days.

Before transferring to our camp compound within the park, Alfred decided to give us an impromptu tour of his community including showing us where he and his family lived and offering us a welcome drink at his brother's bar all the time filling us with stories of how the people lived. This was the real Africa we had come to see!

South Africa is a beautiful country of extreme wealth and poverty with a very small middle class. The government has enacted legislation to empower blacks. Black economic empowerment is a policy that requires all companies that do business with the government to have a majority of blacks in their employment. Thus you have white legal firms hiring newly graduated black lawyers so that they will be eligible for government work. Many whites, discouraged by lack of opportunities, have emigrated elsewhere.

Alfred and his family are of the new middle class in South Africa and he is rightly proud of all he has accomplished. After a cursory tour of the park, Alfred took us to our compound, which was to be our residence for the next three days. Having made arrangements with a Cape Town travel agency, we were pleasantly surprised at the modest yet totally functional African huts that the agent had arranged. Each hut had two single beds, washroom-shower with hot and cold water, and a small kitchen unit all totally air-conditioned. A food store, restaurant, swimming pool and recreation area were within the compound protected from the wild animals by an electric perimeter fence wire. We shared our compound with many South African families but not a single foreign tourist.

The wealthy foreign tourists, like the couples who shared our van, were taken to five-star camps that cost up to $1,000 a night. When asked where he would stay Alfred showed us his tent trailer located within our compound. We were told we would be having an early 5 a.m. start. Exhausted from the day's activities we immediately fell asleep in bed.

At the time promised Albert gave a gentle knock at our door. After a quick breakfast we were off on safari. As we started our journey in search of wildlife the air was calm, the sky misty and a sense of peace and tranquility defied description. We were at one with nature. Not five minutes later we came upon a ground party about to hike through the forest. Albert, who knew the armed guides, stopped to say hello. After declining their gracious invitation to join them we were told that if animals intimidated the tourists they would be shot. A policy I'm not entirely sure I agree with.

It soon became apparent that Alfred was a true expert at what he did. Always learning the natural habitat of the animals, being able to read their footprints and feces enabled him to track and find them. Thus we were blessed to see a pride of lions as they digested the previous night's meal only three metres from our truck. Thankfully Alfred's wildlife skill included knowing the signs when an animal would attack. We spotted two rare white rhinoceros sleeping on a bank. Impalas, giraffes, monkeys, wild dogs, beautiful zebras, and a herd of water buffalo all were seen during that first day

Normally safaris consist of a three-hour drive in the early morning and a two-hour drive late in the afternoon with some operators adding a short evening tour. That first day the boys and I were a total of 14 hours in the jeep. We drove the entire length of the park from our campsite to areas bordering Mozambique and Zimbabwe. During our three days we saw the big five many times. They are so named because they are the most difficult for the big game hunter to kill. They are the elephant, lion, rhinoceros, water buffalo and leopard.

The beauty and magnificence of Kruger National Park is a once-in-a-life time experience. The highlight of our safari came early that first morning when Alfred spotted a leopard stalking an impala. We watched the leopard, which is capable of running 100 kilometres an hour, hiding in the bush patiently waiting to see if an impala would come close enough for it to make the kill. This was a real live cat-and-mouse game. Fortunately for the impala it lived to see another day.

During the next two days we went on three more prolonged drives, always seeing something of interest. Foreign tourists on safaris are mostly whites from Europe and North America and for the most part well behaved. However, white South Africans are a different matter often cutting in and placing their cars directly in line with the animals without concern for fellow humans waiting to see the animals. The guides, on the other hand, have a sense of sharing and community wonderful to behold. Often the guides would radio each other if a rare animal was spotted, telling on-going car drivers to not stay too long so that others could get their turn and above all taking an enormous pride in the natural beauty of their park.

A final note about Alfred, our humane and compassionate guide, who at one point stops the jeep to pick up a turtle stranded on the road and carry it to safety. Alfred wants to expand his Lutheran church and requires a computer.

After flying to Cape Town with my children, I had the privilege the next morning to tour Robben Island, a 45-minute boat ride away. The island, 12 kilometres in circumference, was first used for slaves by the Dutch in 1658 and later in the 1800s became a leper colony. During South Africa's apartheid policies of the 1960s the island became infamous for its political prisoners. Nelson Mandela, later to become the first black president of South Africa, was a political prisoner on the island from 1964-1982. Visiting Mandela's 2x3 metre cell, with it metal bed and bucket for a toilet, is truly a humbling experience. Our tour guide, a former political prisoner, told us a typical day started at 5 a.m. with eight hours of hard labour in the nearby limestone quarry. Supper at 4.30 p.m. was followed by school or political meetings in the central courtyard. It was the fervour of their beliefs that enabled many of the prisoners to survive to see the majority ruled independent state of South Africa. Mandela was a natural leader, lawyer and a gentle and spiritual man whom the guards admired and respected. They are said to have often asked him for advice on their own personal problems.

South Africa, a country of 40 million people, 80 per cent black and with 11 different languages, has a well-educated and influential Jewish community. I took the time to visit the Jewish museum and Holocaust memorial in Cape Town. At its peak 120,000 Jews lived in South Africa. Currently the population is 90,000. Many have left to live in Israel, New Zealand and Canada.

The history of the Jews in South Africa goes back to the beginning of the state in the 1800s when Lithuanian and Russian Jews came via boat from London. The first synagogues were established in the 1840s. Many Jews started merchant careers as peddlers to the diamond and gold industries.

More recently the Jews had a strong affinity with the African National Congress (ANC) and with Nelson Mandela. Many civil rights lawyers who represented the ANC were Jews. One female Jewish MP actively spoke out against the apartheid policies and was a close personal friend of Mandela. Like many other educated and professional whites many of the Jews seek a more stable and secure country to raise their families.

South Africa is a country of contrasts. It is said that South Africa is both a third world and a first world country and you never know which to expect. I had the privilege of touring the townships near Cape Town, which in time of segregation kept blacks far away from whites in the cities and close to the farms where they served as cheap labour. The townships, some as large as a million people strong, have their own sets of strata. The wealthy live in large modern homes with all conveniences while others, lower in the strata, live in huts without electricity or running water. Education, health issues and high unemployment are major issues the government is faced with.

The next day, by happenstance, I was scheduled to play golf with my sons, and a black English neighbour at the Jewish golf course, The King David, located a few kilometres from the townships. What a contrast in worlds. Surrounded by a security fence and guards we entered a world of wealth and privilege. Being at the King David is like living in British colonial times with black servants at beck and call ready to meet any need.

Weakened by a virus, I struggled both physically and golf wise to keep up with my fit and athletic partners. However, on the back nine, with the assistance of a caddy, I miraculously found my game and had a most enjoyable day. That was about to change. On the way out our car would not start. A simple boost from a worker and we were on our way.

Not five minutes later on the freeway the engine suddenly died out and miraculously my son's neighbour steered it to the side of the road not 20 metres from the township I had visited the day before. Out of the car we stumbled, three whites and a black man. All of us had left our cell phones at home. During the next 10 minutes that felt like the longest 10 minutes of my life we desperately tried to wave for help, knowing no one would be foolish enough to stop in a crime infested zone metres away from the township. Suddenly a police car with three officers on their way to work came to our rescue. After radioing in to their captain they were told not to leave us alone and to stay with us no matter how long it took for the tow-truck to arrive.

During the next 90 minutes we were entertained by one of the officers who told us stories of crime fit for the *Tonight Show*. He told us of a middle-aged woman who had been arrested repeatedly for public drunkenness. When she was hospitalized other criminals put together a fund so that she could get private health care. Other stories involved inappropriate calls to the police including people looking for the weather forecast and a man looking for his lost cat. The police officer also told us that when they first came upon us they thought it funny that three white guys were robbing a black man. Thankful for our narrow escape we insisted on sending supper to their precinct. I also wrote a letter to the editor of the local paper, *The Cape Times*, praising the virtues of the Cape Town police

The Editor/Cape Times,
Cape Town, 8000

Dear Sir/Madam

> *As a recent visitor from Canada to your magnificent city I was made aware of the high crime and poverty issues endemic to Cape Town and Africa in general. Today, after returning from a golf outing, our car suffered a complete mechanical breakdown, resulting in all family members being stranded without access to a cell phone on the N1 highway close to the townships. To say I was frightened is to underestimate our vulnerability. Fortunately three police officers, on their way to the Camp Bay station, stopped and waited over an hour with us before we were mobilized. The officers' acts represent to me basic human sensitivity, connectiveness and respect. This augurs well for the future of this country. On behalf of myself and my family, I thank them for their professionalism and most compassionate and thoughtful response.*

> *Yours sincerely*
> *David Nozick*

The next day I saw another act of humanity. A blind elderly white man was struggling to cross the road and a young black man immediately came to his rescue.

Visiting South Africa was an exhilarating and exhausting experience that stretched my comfort level to the maximum. Allowing me to go beyond my comfort zone resulted in an experience of tremendous growth and enlightenment. It made me more aware of the plight of others and the need for community and fellowship.

South Africa is like an adolescence struggling to find her identity. At times she exhibits true maturity as a nation; other times she exhibits selfish childlike behaviour. Let us hope this rainbow nation truly finds her role as the leader of the African continent.

LIFE'S LESSON—*We are all our brothers' keepers. Do not be afraid to stretch your comfort zone.*

CHAPTER 15

---◆---

IN THE HOLY LAND

I have been blessed to visit the State of Israel on three separate occasions. After successfully completing a series of one-year contracts with the federal government, I was awarded a two-year contract that was abruptly terminated for reasons of cost containment. I was told I had no legal basis for a settlement. Nevertheless, with the help of my lawyer friend, I was able to successfully negotiate a sizable severance package.

With this new source of riches I decided to fulfil a lifetime dream of seeing Israel, visiting my youngest son who was spending a year on a kibbutz in the Negev desert. Arriving at Ben Gurion Airport, I stepped off the plane to a hot, hazy sky filled with the calming aroma of eucalyptus. Kissing the ground, I truly felt I had come home. As I checked through passport control I was amazed at the vast array of Jews arriving from all corners of the world.

Moshe, a burly former infantry solder was my bus driver to my hotel in Jerusalem. I learned first hand why more Israelis are killed on the highways of Israel than all the solders killed in the wars Israel has fought. I arrived at the hotel in 45 minutes. My thoughts were of the calmness of my transatlantic flight compared with the unruly traffic.

After checking into my hotel at 7 a.m., I had five hours to pass before my scheduled rendezvous with my son. I was in the lobby contemplating my next move when an orthodox man of slight stature who seemed non-threatening greeted me. He turned out to be a history professor from America who had made aliyah (return to Israel) and was looking to earn extra money as a tour guide. Divine providence had provided me what I needed in Jerusalem.

After a fascinating tour of old Jerusalem it was hard to accept I was actually there. How to describe one's emotions standing at the Wailing Wall, the remnants of the wall of the Second Temple and the most important site for religious and secular Jews alike, is a difficult task. To actually write a note and, like millions of others before me to physically place that note in one of the crevices of the wall, is to feel if only temporary at one with G-d.

At that moment it was easy to understand a strange phenomenon unique to Jerusalem called the Jerusalem psychoses, characterized by euphoria so intense that people literally lose temporary contact with reality. Time passed quickly and before I knew it I was deposited back at my hotel. Imagine my delight when I entered my hotel room to find my eighteen year old son, Daniel, fast asleep in my bed.

After my son and I had a chance to get caught up with each other's lives, I decided we would celebrate a traditional event in Jerusalem. We would attend a *shabbos* dinner being held that night at the hotel. What a beautiful evening we spent with strangers who fast became friends at a traditional Friday service and meal. The sense of community and fellowship that we experienced is known to Jews all over the world and was for me a marvelous start to a soul-searching and life-altering journey.

The next day I meet fellow travelers, significantly reduced because of the infidel. This diverse group of North America Jews would gradually merge over the next two weeks into a dynamic and closely-knit family.

Without question the highlight of the trip was visiting the West Bank, home to many biblical sites. Touring Bethlehem, with my youngest son part of the group, was a wonderful opportunity to meet the people of the West Bank without the politics. As Jews in an Arab land, we felt most welcomed in Bethlehem, the birthplace of Jesus. It was to my mind a moving and humbling experience for both believer and non-believer alike. Somehow you feel a special sense of reverence and piety that defies description.

Traveling through the West Bank one becomes aware of the tremendous discrepancy between the Arabs and the Jewish settlers. We saw Bedouin tribes living in tents in the desert much like their ancestors many years ago. One concession to modern times was to see the Bedouins tap into a water pipe running through the desert. We also saw Arabs living in substandard conditions in villages next to Jewish settlers living with all the modern conveniences. It is no wonder that the Arabs resent their neighbours

Arriving at Jericho, one of the oldest cities in the world, was an especially poignant moment because of a frightening incident. Our bus, clearly identified Israeli by distinctive yellow license plates, was moving slowly and deliberately through the old town, when suddenly out of the corner of my eye I saw Arab teenagers throwing rocks at cars and buses. It seemed like divine intervention but somehow I instinctively put my hand up to protect my face and the window adjacent to me shattered into a million pieces. Miraculously I emerged without a scratch.

The tour guide and bus driver immediately pulled away to safety. After inquiring about my health the window was temporarily repaired and we continued with our tour. For me, this incident made me aware of the real life of Israelis, and of the personal sacrifices each and every Israeli family has made to the course of peace. In some small way, at least for the moment, I felt at one with my people.

We proceeded due north and soon found ourselves on a kibbutz on Israeli's border with Lebanon. Looking out from my bedroom window I could see the remnants of an old Israeli border station no longer in use. It was a poignant reminder of the troubles that have existed between these two nations and to me a welcome to the political cauldron of the Middle East.

The next evening the group was invited to participate in a special ceremony honouring the solders that have died in the many wars Israel has fought since her birth in 1948. Unfortunately, I missed the bus and spent hours alone walking the grounds of the kibbutzim. Perhaps because the ceremony was taking place I felt a spiritual connection to the people that literally brought me to tears. It was as if I was a small insignificant Jew from Ottawa, who somehow felt in harmony with G-d and with G-d's chosen people.

Remarkably on two other separate visits to Israel I have had similar spiritually awakenings. On my second trip I had the pleasures of visiting my son's kibbutz located in the Western Negev desert close to the tumultuous and politically explosive Gaza strip. Indeed, at the time I was young and brave and chose to drive to my son's kibbutzim from Tel Aviv. Despite detailed instructions I got lost some three kilometres from Gaza. Fortunately, I realized my mistake and successfully negotiated my way to the kibbutz without incident.

My son's kibbutz was a delightful oasis after the hustle and bustle of touring Israel. Here I was able to share a small room with him, dine communally and hear firsthand from members of the kibbutz how they had survived and prospered in a modern Israel. Like all kibbutz that initially relied on an agricultural economy, this kibbutz had progressed to making blankets in an ultra-modern plant with wool imported from New Zealand.

My third trip to Israel was to attend my eldest son's wedding in the old town of Jaffa, near Tel Aviv. Two instances told me I was in G-d's hands and he would take good care of me. First I awoke early one morning and decided I wanted to go to Jerusalem. I was able to book a tour guide who was immediately available and within 60 minutes my family and I were walking through the old city. We were literally glued to the guide. The guide told us that if we did not show fear the Arab shopkeepers would treat us with respect.

Similarly the next day in a taxi to my son's wedding the cab driver, either by mistake or because he was annoyed with us because we would not hire him for our next excursion, let us off in a rather isolated part of Jaffa that felt unsafe. Stuck on a road miles from our destination we felt scared and shaken. Suddenly a car with Israeli license plates stopped. It was a doctor on his way to an emergency. Seeing our predicament he graciously drove us to the wedding minutes before the ceremony was to start. Was it divine intervention, chance or serendipity? You decide.

LIFE'S LESSON—*Do not give up hope no matter how desperate your predicament.*

CHAPTER 16

WRITING

As a seasoned clinical psychologist some of my daily responsibilities are to write psychological reports, consultation notes and various feedback reports. In addition, I have written several professional articles. However, I have never considered myself to be a writer.

Soon after my 50th birthday, I was asked by a local community newspaper to submit a professional article. I suggested I would be willing to do a piece on what it meant for me to turn 50. I wrote the article but was unhappy with the edited version. Nevertheless, I received considerable positive feedback that encouraged me to continue my writing. I have taken the liberty of enclosing the original version of my first article.

PERSONAL REFLECTIONS ON TURNING 50

I am many things to many people as a practising clinical psychologist. However, who I am and how I see myself is a result of my own internal debate and journey of life. As a product of both the silent generation and baby-boomer generation, like so many of my peers, I have acquired a well-defined set of Jewish moral and ethical values that have served me well as I "climbed the corporate ladder" and raised a family.

During those early years, life seemed well defined and relativity simple. Being a natural caretaker and caregiver, I chose to opt into the society my parents gave me. This, for a man of my generation meant being a good provider, taking care of the "outside of the house" and being there for my family. Later, the women's movement, children's rights, massive changes in immigration policies, technological advances and economic patterns would contribute to the confusion between the roles of men and women.

This smooth period of my life was suddenly interrupted at the age of 40 with what many men experience as a mid-life or identity crisis. Interestingly, most women do not usually experience this phenomenon, having already had their own internal debate years earlier regarding their nurturing role versus maintaining their professional careers. As is common with people experiencing an identity crisis, I questioned everything about my life including my values, self-worth and life goals. The next decade of my life would go a long way in attempting to answer those questions.

Despite the fact my generation is one of the wealthiest, healthiest and most privileged, during our forties all of us have had to deal with issues no one is ever prepared for. Each of us must cope with losses, whether it is due to health, death, divorce or loss of jobs. Perhaps, for the first time in our lives, we experience our vulnerability to pain and/or loss.

How we handle our losses, whether we allow ourselves the time to mourn and to heal, or if we choose to remain stuck in our anger, will determine the manner in which we live out the rest of our lives. Each of us must learn to open ourselves to our support systems and allow others the privilege of caring for us.

Many have written of the differences between men and women but with age and grace comes integration, where each of the sexes becomes more in touch with traits of the opposite sex. Thus many men display the wonderful feminine attributes of sensitivity, nurturing and bonding whereas women become more self-confident, assertive and goal-directed. These new found traits which are commonly found as one reaches one's fifties lead to more equal and satisfying relationships.

As I approach the autumn of my life, there is a sense of renewal and purpose, a spiritual reawakening that allows me to accept my limitations and to cherish the daily miracles. Although I value external stimulation and beauty, it is the inner peace and strength that carry me forward. I have redefined my goals to include closer relations with my family, children, loved ones, clients and friends. I have a need to encourage the youth of today, whether it is professionally or as a mentor or friend, with their struggle to seek their identity in this constantly changing world. I have taken on new challenges and am striving to understand the massive technological and sociological changes that are occurring in society.

Although I have chosen to write this essay in a personal format, these changes I have attempted to articulate in my own growth are similar to other men and women who have taken the time and energy to get to know themselves on their journey of life.

As an immediate consequence of that article, I caught the writing bug. Those of you who enjoy the written word will know the euphoria of being able to express inner feeling and thoughts. I began to write articles of a human interest and submitted them to various publications. To my surprise, I received an invitation to serve on the editorial board of a local community paper with the privilege of writing a column. My first column was a poorly disguised tribute to Jason. The article, entitled *Some Men Don't Get It*, was interpreted in different ways. A close personal friend worried that I was not getting enough sex.

"Through my professional life, I have had the opportunity to observe and interpret man's behaviour in this increasingly pluralistic, multicultural and highly technical society.

Simply stated some men do not get it. Our fathers' generation knew their role in society. All male responsibilities were located outside the home and inside was the domain of our mothers.

Our children, on the other hand, have mastered the skill of communication, negotiation and flexibility and have learned to balance their lives in a more meaningful way. No longer is a man simply committed to his job but now is intimately involved as an equal partner in raising his children. Simply stated, our sons get it.

According to David Foote, professor of economics at the University of Toronto and author of the widely read Boom, Bust and Echo, demographic shifts serve as the primary explanation of a myriad of social changes that have occurred in Canada over the past several decades.

Today, early baby boomers are in the midst of a demographic shift while becoming grandparents and facing declining resources, a situation that is totally unfamiliar to them. No longer do they occupy the seats of power and influence. These men have become confused in this new and complicated society. Perhaps instead of looking to our fathers' generation, we need to learn from our sons.

Men of our sons' generation are not caught up in the rat race. Their identity does not depend on the size of their pay cheques. Instead, they have learned to value relationships of all kinds. They are better husbands, fathers and friends because they have learned that actions speak louder than words. They spend time and energy in activities designed to enhance these relationships.

What of my generation of men? What has led us to such confusion? Is it fear and discontent? We, of the early baby boomers, are now approaching our sixties and with it come thoughts of retirement, feelings of mortality and loss of certain functions. Previous macho and competitive behaviours, whether in our professions, business activities or recreational pursuits, are now waning as we realize perhaps for the first time that we cannot compete with the stronger and younger generation.

Essentially, we are left with two choices. One choice is to continue on the path we have been socially trained by our fathers. That is to face our declining resources with renewed efforts to remain competitive and relevant in today's society. Such a man, despite his best efforts, wonders what he did that results in family members and friends feeling increasingly alienated and misunderstood. He is unable to understand the loss of his power in all aspects of his life and remains confused and feeling incompetent and irrelevant.

What of those who have chosen the second path, who have attempted to make the changes necessary to become more enlightened and aware of our declining resources? This man, now approaching retirement, realizes the path to fulfillment is not one espoused by our fathers, but that it is to the role models of our sons that we must turn to.

What have our sons taught us? First, that their identity is not linked to power or control but to developing, nurturing, loving and more equitable relationships. It is no longer valid for men to dominate and control.

We men of a certain generation need to be more in contact with our sensitive feminine side that allows us to listen more intensely and to be more in touch with our feelings. It is precisely these attributes that will lead men to fulfillment, inner peace and love in their declining years."

Unfortunately, the paper I was writing for recently changed ownership and with it came a new editorial board that has gone in a different direction.

Having lost my public voice, I searched for ways to express myself. It was as if I had this inner need to write and comment on life. I happened upon an ad in the paper about a basic journalistic writing course at the local community college in Ottawa. The course teaches participants about writing for the media. Initially, I thought it was a general interest course, however, when I attended my first class—and found myself among students younger than my children and the instructor outlining the requirements of the course—I quickly realized I had registered in a credit course. What a dilemma, could my fragile ego handle the pressure of formal education not as a professor but as a lowly student!

In addition to the writing assignments the course emphasized the *Canadian Press Stylebook* for writing, grammar and spelling. These are subjects I have always struggled with because of my auditory perception difficulties.

As I wrestled around whether to commit myself to the rigours of formal education, not having been in the classroom for more than 30 years, a few students dropped out of the course. But I decided this might be an opportunity to improve my writing and get professional feedback from the professor and I reluctantly stayed in.

During the next 15 weeks I entered the class with mixed emotions. I thoroughly enjoyed the professor's (a former award-winning journalist) insights, perceptions and experiences. On the other hand I found the weekly word usage and spelling quizzes absolutely terrifying! There was no hiding behind my PhD or professional accomplishments. I was simply a student who had to study and do hard work. And study I did as I dusted off all the old tricks of the trade that enabled me to obtain my PhD more than 35 years previous. I pleasantly surprised myself by obtaining a final Grade A-. What follows is one of my class assignments.

THE JOYS OF PASSPORT RENEWAL

Awakening early one morning, not to the passport office but to the post office where a colleague promised there would be no line-up. Indeed, as promised at 8:30 a.m., there was no line and also no one to serve me. The lady, whose job it is to serve Canadian passport applications, was due to arrive at 9:15 a.m.

Being a courteous and law-abiding Canadian citizen, I proudly took my place at the head of the line and then waited, all the time conversing quietly—in the Canadian way—with my peers. At exactly 9:15 a.m., the passport lady greeted me and duly noted that since my passport was needed within 45 days, it would not be possible to process the application where I was. Instead, she recommended I go to the main passport office downtown.

As a resident of Ottawa, home of the federal government, it is considered wise to take the advice of official Ottawa. Failure to do so often results in untimely delays or worse. Some cases have literally disappeared into the bowels of official Ottawa, never again to see the light of day.

Arriving at the main Ottawa passport office, a long queue snaked through the corridor. The commissioner on duty, a friendly type, remarked: "The entire process will take less than one hour, significantly less time than the nine hour wait in Vancouver." Passively taking my place at the end of the line, I noticed two individuals whom I had seen earlier at the post office. They now enjoyed the privilege of being ahead of me in the queue. A by-product of queuing with like-minded Canadians is to be made aware of the various war stories associated with passport renewal. Little did I know that I would soon become one of them.

After serving my allocated time, the clerk charged with verification of my documents indicated there was a problem. Would I mind waiting while she consulted with her supervisor? After what seemed like hours, the sweat pouring out of orifices I did not know I had, I approached the clerk who informed me I would not be getting a new passport that day. It seems in my haste to renew my passport, I had misread the date of expiry and I had more than a year left. The cost to me: A severely bruised ego, public humiliation and a few hours of my life. On a more positive note, I found out the process was fair, equitable and provided a unique opportunity to meet fellow Canadians. It was a wonderful dress rehearsal for when my passport truly needs renewal.

Having successfully completed the course, I learned that 60 is really only a number and that despite the passage of time I was still capable of acquiring new skills. With my renewed confidence, I continued my search to perfecting my writing skills. Once again my eye caught an advertisement regarding a course offered by the local school board. It was a general interest course entitled *Is Your Story Interesting to Write About?* The seminar was led by Susan Jennings, a woman who had written a beautiful book about her own survival story. The seminar was especially helpful to me in that it served to help me get unstuck.

For years I had wanted to write a book, but felt lost on how to start it. During discussions with Susan, I learned that it is not necessary to proceed chronologically but often advisable to start in the middle. It is precisely this insight that has enabled me to proceed with this narrative. This manuscript is a direct by-product of that seminar and I will eternally be grateful to Susan Jennings's inspirational role model.

During the process of writing this manuscript I have had occasion to seek guidance and wisdom from men and women I highly respect. One such gentleman was Arnie, whose impressive biography I described previously. Arnie, in his own distinctive way, was both encouraging and critical. After considerable reflection and filtering I decided to incorporate his suggestions into the text. I thank him for being a true friend for telling it like it was.

LIFE'S LESSON—*Seek advice from trusted friends. Put away your ego and filter carefully what they say. If your sixth sense tells you it is right, incorporate the lesson into your being and celebrate your personal growth.*

CHAPTER 17

—◆—

MENTORS I HAVE KNOWN

During my career, I have met many distinguished and capable men
and women whose exemplary lives have served to inspire me to be a
better person. One such man was the Honourable Justice Sam Freedman,
Chancellor of the University of Manitoba.

After obtaining my BSc degree my father suggested as a way of
enhancing my application to medical school that I contact Mr. Freedman,
the Chief Justice of Manitoba, for a character reference. Mr. Freedman
was a friend of the family and arranged to meet me at his office. This
event more than 40 years ago is firmly etched in my memory. I entered
this unbelievably beautiful oak-walled room lined with books everywhere.
Behind a massive desk sat this rather petite man who spoke to me in a soft,
almost inaudible voice.

He invited me to sit across from him and talked to me about how
our families had known each other. He also showed a keen interest in my
career plans. It was as if I was talking to my own grandfather. I left feeling
a sense of euphoria and with a highly prized character reference.

However, it was not until years later that I fully understood the
greatness, the humanity and the total sense of humility that this man
exuded despite occupying one of the most influential seats of power in
Manitoba. I considered myself fortunate to have met a truly great Canadian
and to this day keep an original copy of that letter

November 9, 1966.

To Whom It May Concern

                    Re: David Nozick,
                          422 Boreham Boulevard,
                          Tuxedo, Manitoba.

          Mr. David Nozick obtained his Bachelor
of Science Degree from the Univeristy of Manitoba
in 1966. He is presently a pre-Masters student in
Psychology at this University.

          Because he is particularly interested
in Industrial Psychology — a course of study not
given at this University — he is planning to seek
admission, as of September 1967, in the Masters course
in Psychology at a university where such course is
available. I am pleased to write this letter in
support of his application.

          I have known Mr. Nozick for several
years, as I am a friend of his parents. I know that
in the past two years of his course he was an Honours
student with an average of about 70%. I have no
doubt that his academic performance will be attested
to by others more qualified than I to speak in that
area. What I should like to offer is a testimonial
to this student's personal qualifications — of mind
and of character. This is a young man of great
dependability and with a deep determination to get
ahead in the field which he has selected for himself.
He is considering a teaching career as his ultimate
goal and I feel he would do well in it.

          I am happy to commend his application
to your favourable consideration.

                              Yours truly,

                              Samuel Freedman

                    Mr. Justice Samuel Freedman

I shall speak of two mentors in my chosen field who have served as role models to me. In turn, I have shared my knowledge with many budding psychologists in the community, something I find particularly gratifying and rewarding.

I first met Mo in 1968, soon after obtaining my Master's Degree in Psychology from the University of Manitoba. My first job after graduation was as a school psychologist with the Winnipeg School Division at the princely salary of $6,800 a year. At the age of 22, recently married, I was hired to tend to the psychological needs of school-aged children. Although psychotherapy was part of my mandate, the principle function of the school psychologist was to diagnosis children with learning, behavioural, and emotional difficulties.

I worked first in the inner city, dealing primarily with children from disadvantaged families. The previous summer the city of Winnipeg's office for re-registering welfare recipients had employed me. Both experiences helped me appreciate the barriers disadvantaged families face to meet their basic needs and provide for their families.

The following year I was promoted to work in the suburbs. This would prove to be an altogether different set of challenges. One such challenge was being asked to provide service to a family who knew my biological family. When the mother of the child involved called me *Duddie*, a nickname known only to my closest family, it was clear another psychologist would better serve her.

As one of the young bucks at the Child Guidance Clinic (CGC), I was a member of a rather dynamic professional group of young men who were eager to learn and advance. As such, we met often after work hours to go over various protocols and to learn from each other. The fearless leader of this group was Mo, the official head of the psychological department. Unofficially, Mo occupied the role of shit disturber and rebel. Mo was a man in his late forties, a Cape Bretonner who migrated west to Toronto to study for his PhD in clinical psychology. After aborting his studies he settled in Winnipeg where he became a legend in the field of psychology.

Soon after my arrival at CGC, I was subject to supervision by a competent senior psychologist. A year later, I asked and was granted the privilege to be supervised by Mo. The change gave me an entirely different work experience.

Although we did the usual stuff of going over protocols and discussing cases, it felt more like a lesson in life. No topic was out of bounds, including one's personal life or values. Mo would challenge you on almost everything you did or did not do. It felt like going through a meat grinder and you were happy to have survived. One benefit was you grew enormously both as a psychologist and person.

Mo was simply the best damn psychologist I ever met. He was analytical, perceptive, insightful, highly articulate, energetic and passionate about the study of psychology. Here was a man who clearly loved what he was doing and he had the gift of infusing all of us privileged to work with him with the same enthusiasm. Three hours of supervision a week with Mo proved to be the highlight of my career. Any competency or reputation I now enjoy as a psychologist is directly related to being trained by him. Thank you, Mo, for being there for me and helping me to become the person I am today.

Mo had many redeeming qualities, not the least his desire to talk endlessly. During one staff meeting he was going on and on about something. I, then a brash 22-year-old, stood up at the back of the room and shouted: "Mo, time is money". For the first time in his life Mo came to an immediate stop. Silence followed. When I later visited Mo in Winnipeg, he proudly reminded me of the words of his **protégée**.

Mo was a source of inspiration and a surrogate father to me. He was a man I admired greatly for his clinical skills and more importantly for how he handled adversity. Mo, and his then wife, had the onerous responsibility of raising three severely challenged children. He looked upon it as a blessing. Similarly, his divorce and ultimately his last combat with colon cancer, were fought with dignity and courage.

Mo was my mentor, friend, and colleague and I miss him dearly. He was there for me when I truly needed him. I feel privileged to have known him and thank him for the lessons of life. In honour of Mo, I have named this book after a Latin phrase that Mo signed off on all his letters. It is a phrase I proudly teach to every one of my clients:

NON ILLIGITAMUS CARBORUNDUM

(Don't Let the Bastards Wear You Down)

After spending 2½ years studying for my PhD at the University of Ottawa, financial considerations dictated that I should seek employment.

On October 15, 1972, after extensive negotiations with Dr. B had ended, I agreed to begin my clinical career in Ottawa as a school psychologist. The negotiations had centred on having enough time to complete my dissertation, as I was determined not to be one of *them,* a PhD without thesis who failed to complete the final requirements of the degree.

Postponing the start of my career by six weeks proved to be a brilliant decision as I was literally forced to work night and day to complete my dissertation. As a school psychologist, I reported directly to Dr. B, an elegant, compassionate and extremely sophisticated woman. This was my first experience working directly for a woman boss. But not any woman! Dr. B, who with her first husband had been a prominent member of the diplomatic corps in Washington, was a woman who literally moved mountains to make things happen.

In my entire career I have never seen a person work a room like she did. Dr. B would slowly talk to each and every person in the room as if they were the only one there. Each person felt they had her complete and undivided attention. She had a gift for listening, understanding and for extracting information, often of a personal nature, that strangers somehow felt safe to tell her. After making a cursory tour of a room, Dr. B knew everyone's first name, their children's names, why they were there and their associations with the organization. To see Dr. B in action was a sight to behold. During the 10 years I worked with her we developed a close relationship. She taught me the art of diplomacy and how to achieve a win-win situation with neither party losing face.

I recall one situation when a principal had inappropriately commented on the poor state of my footwear. Being from a family of lawyers, I was ready to do battle. Somehow, Dr. B restored calm and order and defused the situation; once again showing me firsthand the value of diplomacy.

Dr. B was a supportive mentor who wanted the best for her protégés. When I decided to enter my name as a candidate for the director of psychology at a major teaching hospital, Dr. B was firmly behind me. I am convinced that my success in obtaining that position was directly related to her influence.

I must say that not all of Dr. B's ideas were positive. For reasons I have never understood, she chose to schedule staff meetings on Fridays at 3 p.m. and the meetings often ran well into early evening. Staff members were put in a difficult position, needing to be with their family yet not wanting to offend Dr. B or any invited guest. I promised myself if I ever found myself as the head of anything that I would never schedule a staff meeting on a Friday afternoon. A promise I have religiously kept.

LIFE'S LESSON—The Three of Jainism

Right belief, right knowledge, right conduct. These are all the ethics there are. The rest is nonsense.

CHAPTER 18

─────◆─────

THE REAL HEROES

One of the purposes of this book is to acknowledge my privilege to serve my clients over a 39-year career. I have met countless clients who have demonstrated incredible strength of character and fortitude in at first acknowledging and then transforming their transgressions to become better citizens of society.

I have been able to see the inner core of men and women from all walks of life, some educated and powerful, others from more modest circumstances, but all with a willingness to walk into my office and bare their souls. I give thanks for allowing me to be a part of their personal journey and hopefully helping them understand themselves in order to live a more meaningful and purposeful life.

Truth be told, my clients are my real heroes for facing head-on their pain and suffering and somehow managing to cope, grow and ultimately to become more actualized as the person they want to be.

I want to publicly acknowledge what I have inwardly known for a long time, namely, that clients are not seen in a vacuum. They have a tremendous impact on the lives of their helpers. Just as it is true that clients develop and grow, it is equally true that therapists who are open to life's experiences also benefit greatly from client experiences and insights.

Every therapist, doctor, minister or social worker has at least one client who is at the same time the most challenging as well as the most rewarding. For me, it will always be Louise. I have known Louise for more than thirty-five years. I first met her in October of 1972 when I was a rookie school psychologist at the Ottawa Board of Education and she was an angry seventeen year-old student who gave her teachers all sorts of grief.

At the time I first saw her, I was a married man who had just become a father and was in the final stages of completing my PhD in clinical psychology. With the exception of the loss of my parents and my unexpected divorce, I have lived a charmed and privileged life. Louise, on the other hand, had been subjugated to abuse and traumas too numerous to mention that would have destroyed a lesser woman. Despite our separate journeys our lives have many similarities. It seems with perseverance, compassion, respect and dignity both of us managed to cross a field strewn with life's landmines and enter a place where inner peace, tranquility and a sense of self and purpose define our beings.

How can I explain more than 30 years of psychotherapy and more than 1,200 hours of incredible work and dedication on both our parts that helped her deal with the trauma that was so severe that it is a miracle she is still alive today? There were times when Louise was so terrorized that the only way we could conduct therapy was with her standing next to an open door. Somehow I sensed that had I attempted to close that door she would have bolted like an animal running for her life.

It was in 1980 that I entered private practice and placed an announcement in the local paper. As luck would have it, Louise saw the announcement and phoned me to see if I was taking new clients. The rest is history.

Unfortunately, the eight-year interruption between 1972 and 1980 had served to exacerbate her symptoms to such a state that she began to de-personalize, a very scary psychological state known to victims of severe sexual abuse. De-personalization is a state in which individuals separate their emotions from their being by adopting a separate persona. It frightens both client and practitioner. Some clients have an out-of-body experience. They appear to be looking at themselves from above without any emotional content.

I did not know whether Louise could be brought back to reality. On a few occasions, I had to call 911 and have her hospitalized. Despite these setbacks, we persevered and were able to get beyond the trauma and deal with the issues that were germane to her mental health. At the time of writing Louise has regained her strong artistic and humanitarian identity and has decided to fly solo on her life's journey.

Louise has taught me valuable lessons not the least of which are that faith, hope, respect and dignity will win out over abuse, materialism, social status or prejudice. Perhaps the most important lesson Louise taught me is that one person who really gives a damn can make a difference between whether a person makes it or not. Louise is a remarkable woman who has endured hardships no person should have to endure, yet despite it all, she maintains self-respect and dignity. She is a woman who has my utmost admiration.

Another long-term client who I deeply admire is Fred. Some 15 years ago, Fred was looking for a psychologist to help him re-enter the labour market after suffering a psychotic break. Fred's paranoia and anxiety had progressed to such a state that he no longer was in contact with reality. At the time I started seeing Fred, then in his late 30s, he was sufficiently recovered to contemplate returning to work.

Fred, a short man with a slight paunch whose manner of dress and deportment closely resembles the Peter Sellers' character Inspector Clousseau, is a hyperactive individual whose mind and body never seem to stop moving. Often underestimated, Fred's razor-sharp mind offers an encyclopaedia of knowledge. He is well read with an informed opinion on history, philosophy and current events. Despite his impressive IQ, Fred suffers from social anxiety such that normal social interaction is extremely stressful for him. With perseverance Fred was able to obtain a clerical position within the federal government. Fred recently decided to take a medical pension and early retirement.

The challenges dealing with Fred were to understand his extremely analytical thought process and to help him focus and direct his thoughts. A budding painter, writer and Renaissance man, Fred has a huge heart that has helped many of his friends in need. I am indebted to Fred for his insights and observations. Fred helped me put into perspective what is truly important in life. In the Yiddish language of my ancestors, Fred is a true *mensch* and I wish him well in his retirement.

After all is said and done, perhaps the client I most admire is Sam. He is a middle-aged man inflicted with cerebral palsy who uses his wheelchair to travel great distances in all kinds of weather. Somehow, in a howling winter storm when many of my able-bodied clients were cancelling, Sam would appear on time for his appointment.

I first met Sam some 20 years ago when I first entered private practice. He has gifted intelligence but his courage in facing all kinds of limitations is legendary. How not to admire his yearly train trips to Prince Edward Island where he has to arrange a private taxi the last 100 kilometres of his journey!

Until recently Sam was gainfully employed as a computer technician with the federal government. As a result of his decreased mobility, pain and arthritis he was granted a medical pension. He finds it frustrating to retire at such a young age. Sam talks about being a 40-year-old man in a 60-year-old body. Despite his physical limitations Sam could often be found in his wheelchair with a huge smile in the middle of a crowd of people miles from his home. He is a man of enormous charm with a wide array of able-bodied men and women he counts as friends.

A socially gregarious man with a wicked sense of humour, Sam is famous for his collection of memorabilia. A cursory survey of his apartment reveals posters, old-time Coke bottles and numerous artefacts devoted to Coke. I have often told him he would be the perfect spokesperson for Coca-Cola.

Able-bodied people often misunderstand the struggles of physically challenged adults. Many take disabled people as aged and demented and often do not accord them the respect and dignity they deserve. I have seen Sam literally crawl hands and knees to get to a washroom despite the fact there was a wheelchair-accessible washroom on another floor that the occupant refused to share with him because of bureaucratic protocol.

Sam has taught me what it is like to face head on one's limitations. How, despite many setbacks in life, it is possible to maintain one's dignity and self-respect and to live life to the fullest every moment of every day and night. Thank you, Sam, for allowing me the privilege to be a part of your most inspiring life.

I also want to thank the many other clients I have seen whose stories are just as compelling. Unfortunately, time and space does not allow me to detail them here. All of them have shown courage and wisdom

LIFE'S LESSON—*My clients are my real heroes. They gave me the opportunity to learn the real lessons of life.*

CHAPTER 19

VOLUNTEERING

One of the values I was taught is that one is a member of a community and there are certain responsibilities within that community. Thus, if you are playing ice hockey and the synagogue across the street is looking for a 10th man to complete the *minyan* (*Kaddish,* the prayer for the dead), you immediately take off your skates and participate at the synagogue.

Similarly, my parents devoted considerable time and energy to service clubs raising money for various causes. One of the ironies of my life is my father was a member of the Lion's Club, which raised funds for the very institution, Lion's Manor, where my mother spent the last 12 years of her life. Her sojourn there was filled with love that I truly believe extended her life at least 10 years.

Thus voluntarism was a way of life for me. The only question was how, when and where to make a contribution.

During my married life voluntarism took on the role of board member. Being an upperly bound professional with considerable ambition, it was a win-win situation when I agreed to serve on social service boards. Serving on the board gave me the advantage of being able to see the big picture of an organization and to learn the politics and nuances surrounding it. This would later serve me well as I negotiated my way through the maze of hospital administration. An additional perk was to be included in the inner circle of social and community happenings. Thus, while I believe I made a contribution, it was by no means a one-way contract.

During a period when I happened to be on the board of a well known synagogue the Rabbi's contract was up for renewal. The debate whether to renew or not was highly emotional and at times almost totally irrational. Having been elected as a representative of a specific group of the congregation I put aside personal preferences in determining to vote in a manner consistent with my constituency. Lobbying for either yes or no was intense as the direction of the board was not at all clear. The situation was so desperate that ex-presidents of the congregation were entitled to vote; many had one foot in the grave but still made a heroic effort to vote. It was a lesson that would serve me well as a manager and an administrator.

On another occasion I had just recently joined a board of a social agency and within a week was asked to become chairman. Although I was flattered by the invitation, no doubt because of my professional credentials, I felt the learning curve was too steep and politely declined.

During the past 10 years I have continued to volunteer but with a different slant. Perhaps it is because of where I see myself on life's cycle. I am no longer interested in serving on boards. I prefer to be involved with people one on one.

Thus, one fall sunny day I happened to be sauntering through the foyer of City Hall, where various service organizations were displaying their wares in the hope of recruiting volunteers, when I came upon the booth of ELTOC (English Language Training of Ottawa-Carleton). Standing behind the booth was a perky middle-aged woman who immediately engaged me in the virtues of ELTOC, an organisation that trains volunteers to tutor new Canadians in basic English. There are six weeks of orientation training followed by a commitment to work a minimal two hours a week with a student in his or her own home. ELTOC fills the void for immigrants who for one reason or another are unable to take English lessons in a formal classroom setting.

Volunteering is always a win-win situation. During the five years I served with ELTOC, I had the privilege to work with a wonderful man from Afghanistan, an accountant from Peru, and a high-tech couple from China. In each instance we developed a personal friendship. Volunteering allowed me to expand my box of life, to understand the world better as well as encouraging me to travel and see the world.

One particular situation captures the joys and rewards of volunteering. As a Jewish Canadian male, I had the distinct privilege of visiting my Muslim student in his home. Enlightening to me as I parked my car and followed his directions, I came upon the Ottawa Muslim Housing Co-Operative. At the foyer, I rang his apartment, duly entered, and heard the unique call to prayers at the adjacent Mosque. At that moment I truly felt a citizen of the world. Greeted and introduced to my student's family I was treated like a special guest. Thus begin a rewarding and mutually satisfying three-year relationship in which we both learned a great deal about our respective cultures and shared many moments of discovery together. Like most immigrants Mohammed had many tales of survival that truly made me appreciate my Canadian roots.

Several years ago I was looking for something to do and I came upon an advertisement in a community paper to spend time with an elderly gentleman who was confined to his apartment. After the usual vetting, interview, police check and references, the social worker told me not to enter the apartment but to meet my senior in the lobby as his wife was difficult to get on with. Arriving on time, I used the intercom and was told by a commanding male voice to come up to the apartment.

A tall, imposing man, who despite his elderly status seemed youthful, greeted me at the door. I greeted his wife with the traditional *Shabbat Shalom,* and was received in a warm and engaging manner. After clarifying with his support worker when I would bring Bob back, we went for a long car ride, followed by coffee and a return to his apartment. This weekly Saturday morning ritual took place religiously for four years and only ended when Bob was not able to physically negotiate the halls to freedom. During our time together we talked and drank coffee, although I'm sure he would have preferred something stronger, and we drove countless miles through the streets of Ottawa and the neighbouring countryside.

One of Bob's favourite rides was to the top of the Champlain lookout in the Gatineau Hills. From the lookout we had a panoramic view of the entire Ottawa valley. I thought he enjoyed these drives because it reminded him of his Scottish-Irish roots and his professional life as a horticulturist. Often when driving he would provide me with the exact Latin name for a tree or bush we saw along the road. Visiting the federal agricultural grounds, where plant scientists test new species, was always a treat for Bob and me. Bob felt in familiar territory and, at the ripe age of 93, could recall all their names.

Bob had many a yarn to spin from his years as a decorated solder in North Africa and the Middle East. One of my favourites was how he won a medal of distinction for being shot at by friendly fire. The way Bob tells it he was simply trying to get the hell out of the way. Perhaps his best story is how he met his bride of 50 years. He was serving in Israel, what was then Palestine, with the British army. His bride-to-be was a nurse serving with a Jewish service organization. He was assigned to protect her against Arab elements. Bob describes going to her camp in the middle of the night and seeing this apparition with wings that after further view turned out to be the beautiful and talented woman with whom he would share his life.

Bob was a dapper dresser and gracious in his own way. For one thing he always wore this admirable Irish tweed hat and he would always thank me for driving him around with words like: "You'll go to heaven for this." In a sentimental mood one day he wanted to give me his treasured hat. I was touched but could not take it.

Sadly with age Bob became less and less receptive to our outings. Just this past winter I was invited to celebrate his 95th birthday with him and his family. Unfortunately, at the last moment he did not feel well enough to attend.

I will always feel grateful to Bob for allowing me the privilege of being a small part of his life and for sharing with me his wisdom and life experience. Giving has made me more compassionate and caring, affording me the opportunity to meet citizens of the world from all walks of life. I believe this experience has made me a more open and resourceful Canadian.

LIFE'S LESSON—*To give is a privilege and a blessing unto itself.*

CHAPTER 20

MY ROLE AS A STUDENT

"As a child learn good manners, as a young man learn to control your passions, in middle age be just, in old age give good advice and then die without regret."

As an undergraduate science student I was pre-occupied with my goal of becoming a medical doctor and a psychiatrist. For each of us life has those pivotal moments when one comes to a fork in the road and one must choose a direction.

One of my defining moments was when I decided to forego my dream of becoming a medical doctor and pursue a career in clinical psychology. *Chuzpah* (a Yiddish expression meaning nerve or gall) is the only word that describes a 21-year-old *pisher* (Yiddish, meaning young man) with a grand total of two undergraduate courses in psychology deciding to apply for the master's program in psychology at the University of Manitoba.

Somehow, perhaps by divine providence, I was accepted conditionally. That condition, which I successfully met that summer, was to complete the third-year personality course. In today's competitive student world I would not even be considered a qualified candidate. Thus began a long arduous course of studies that ultimately led to my PhD in Clinical Psychology at the University of Ottawa in 1973.

One thing that influenced my decision to pursue my PhD was that Mo, my mentor and friend encouraged me to do so perhaps because he did not finish his. My father offered to take me into the family jewellery business, all the while complaining about how his father had thwarted his plans with the family business. So I might have become a big shot tycoon bedecked in jewellery!

I entered graduate school with the intent of becoming an industrial psychologist at age 21. Finding that the University of Manitoba did not offer such a program I somehow ended up in the field of Experimental Social Psychology. As part of my master's requirement I had to complete a thesis. My thesis topic, *The Self Fulfilling Prophecy*, was a fortunate choice, allowing me to correspond with Harvard's world-renowned psychologist Dr. Robert Rosthenthal. Later, I would parley this topic into a PhD thesis at the University of Ottawa.

After completing my M.A., I worked two exciting and wonderful years at the Child Guidance Clinic in Winnipeg. My work at CGC would provide a solid foundation to my career. I was fortunate to be closely supervised by a highly competent psychologist, followed by the legendary Mo of whom I have spoken. It was not only the excellent supervision but also the collegial atmosphere that encouraged all of us to advance in our profession.

Newly married, with Jason, our eldest son in tow, our family moved to Ottawa after I was accepted into the PhD program. Earlier that summer a friend and I had put my old clunker car on the train to Ottawa. After much searching we found a very practical two-bedroom townhouse for the then princely sum of $175 per month rent. Not until we moved in did I learn the hazards of living adjacent to a low rent housing project. Thus began our family's introduction to the unique cultural and linguistic challenges of living in Ottawa.

Despite our initial setback, Ottawa turned out to be a most inviting community. Soon after we arrived our family was adopted by a family that invited us on *Shabbos* (Friday evening) for a wonderful family meal. Like other newcomers to Ottawa who had come to work for the federal government we soon had a very active social life.

No doubt our transition to Ottawa was eased by fortunate financial circumstances. After inheriting money from my paternal grandfather I was able to parley that into a substantial amount by a very astute financial investment. Coupled with a generous grant I received from the CGC, we started our student life in Ottawa essentially without financial worries.

As a PhD candidate, I faced many known obstacles to acquiring my degree including taking numerous courses, completing a 1,000-hour internship, comprehensive exams and writing a dissertation. I also faced unexpected challenges. PhD candidates are expected to read a professional journal in their field in a second language. Most chose to do it in French.

On the other hand it is an entirely different matter to follow an entire lecture in French. It wasn't the first time that I realized that my high school French didn't cut it. Learning to rely on students more competent in French was a good exercise in learning that no man is an island.

Despite the language issue my greatest challenge at the University of Ottawa, *circa* 1973, was to deal with the internal politics of the psychology department. At the time the department and the university were closely affiliated with the Missionary Oblates of Mary Immaculate (OMI) Order, a Catholic religious order founded on January 25, 1816, by Saint Eugene de Mazenod, a French priest from Marseilles. Although initially focused on working with the poor it became known as a missionary and teaching order as well. The OMI founded the University of Ottawa in 1848. Before then it was known as the College of Bytown. Since 1965 the university has been publicly funded and licensed to grant civil degrees.

During my tenure, 1970-1973, the psychology department was very much under the influence and teachings of the OMI. You can only imagine the shock and emotional reaction of a Jewish student from Winnipeg learning how to deal with most of the professors and the dean who taught from a decidedly Catholic bias. On a practical basis this had a tremendous influence on my internship, clinical supervision and clinical training. Perhaps one example will be sufficient to understand more clearly what I had to face.

As an interning student it soon became apparent that one of the goals of supervision was to strip a student of any sense of self. What transpired was a systematic attempt to spiritually cleanse and transform one into a more humble self-effacing individual in line with Catholic teachings. Not surprising many students resisted this indoctrination. So it was literally the survival of the fittest.

Unfortunately not all of us survived intact. One of my peers whom I was especially fond of suffered a complete mental breakdown. The pressures to conform to expectations yet maintain self-identity were enormous.

Faced with this type of push I turned to fellow students for support and counsel. It felt like being in a bubble isolated from reality. Many suffered breakdowns within families who could not understand the demands being placed upon them. At that time I did not possess the emotional insights or self-confidence to deal effectively with these abusive, controlling and harmful pedagogical methods. Today I would demand that the perpetrators be made accountable. Unfortunately wisdom is often a by-product of the aged. One does not acquire the life skills to cope with difficult circumstances without a long and arduous learning curve.

The third challenge I faced as a PhD candidate was my dissertation. Having previously completed a master's thesis (re-written 13 times) I decided to expand the topic for my PhD. Thus I was able to persuade my thesis adviser and department head to go along with my previous work on non-verbal communication and the self-fulfilling prophecy.

Politely astute, I picked as an advisor a Renaissance professor who was also the department head. He was also both a clinical and experimental psychologist open to new ideas. Coming to his office was always a learning experience whether from his wonderful insights, his comments on life or being privy to his incredible command of language. Thank you, Dr. Bill, for being such a supportive thesis adviser and mentor. How supportive I would learn later at my PhD defence.

In additional to Dr. Bill, I worked closely with a group of internal professors who formed the core of my dissertation committee. Having holed up at the National Library of Canada for more than six months my dissertation proceeded nicely, always going back to the committee before proceeding to the next step. I was determined not to be one of many who did not graduate because they had failed to complete their dissertation. Indeed, my mentor Mo was one of them.

As luck would have it, my internal committee deemed my thesis complete on first draft. The final step, as with all PhDs, is to defend one's thesis before a committee and an external adviser. My adviser generously arranged for me to meet my external adviser from the University of Vermont in his office before proceeding with the formal defence.

I entered my adviser's office and met this warm, kind man who handed me a sheet of questions he was about to ask at the formal defence. I excused myself and went to my sanctuary, the men's washroom, to reflect and analyze my answers. Question 7 jumped off the pages and hit me squarely between the eyes. At first I didn't believe it. I started to shake with limbs totally out of control. Before me was a question that identified a fundamental flaw in my thesis that both the entire internal committee and I had missed and that simply could not be defended by the data.

All people face moral/ethical dilemmas that literally change the direction of their lives. This was one of them. What to do? I had to find a solution on my own.

After considerable thought I decided to stay true to my values. Honesty and integrity are core values for me. Nothing would be gained by trying to bullshit my way out of the situation.

I entered the room calm in the knowledge I would do the right thing. Exactly as promised my external adviser proceeded one by one asking the questions he had indicated. Question 7 was asked and I promptly responded: "You are right there is a fundamental flaw in the design."

Without a second of hesitation he moved on to the next question.

Today I am the proud owner of a PhD in Clinical Psychology because I remained true to my core values.

LIFE'S LESSONS—No matter what the circumstances always be faithful to your core values and you will always be a winner in life.

CHAPTER 21

My Professional Journey

As I wrote earlier clinical psychology was not my first choice as a profession. I had always wanted to be a physician and went so far as to qualify for medicine at the University of Manitoba. Suddenly at the last minute, I decided to pursue clinical psychology. After that initial turn in the road I have never looked back and by any standards have enjoyed a meaningful lifetime career.

Following completion of my PhD studies at the University of Ottawa I was fortunate to be hired by Dr. Bea Wickett, chief psychologist at the Ottawa Board of Education. This amazing diminutive woman was to have a huge influence on my life. The circumstances of my hiring were a good indication of the importance Bea would play. At the time I was first offered a job with the OBE, I had completed all the requirements of my PhD with the exception of my thesis. I refused the initial job offer, only to be inundated with job offers from other agencies. Apparently Bea had heard of my desire to work part time while completing my dissertation and had supported my endeavour. After further negotiations I agreed to come on board six weeks hence thus allowing me to complete the crucial first draft of my thesis.

During my 10 years tenure at the board I diagnosed and treated children and their families from all walks of life. Initially posted to the inner core of the city, I had a chance to work with many ethic families whose culture and values I was not familiar. This offered me an opportunity to expand my knowledge of the world.

My sojourn at the board was filled with many challenges, not the least of which was to deal with the enormous numbers of students who needed to be assessed and treated. Typically, 100 students needed to be seen in a school of 800. Given the limited resources, I was able to visit each school only half days per week with larger high schools given one day per week. Thus it was impossible to respond to all the psychological needs of the students. Waiting lists and referrals to outside agencies helped to stem the flow. As a clinical psychologist who actually enjoyed practising my craft by actually treating clients, I needed to develop a plan that met both my needs and those of the administration. I decided to treat intensely a few select cases, thereby deriving some professional satisfaction.

Constantly facing enormous demands for my services I decided to specialize in family therapy. I prepared myself by taking post-doctoral courses. With the support of the administration a designated family therapy room was built at the board's office. My transformation into a family therapist was one of the most satisfying highlights of my career. During one conference I attended in Cape Cod, colleagues from Harvard, Princeton and Yale surrounded me. Heady stuff for the boy from North End Winnipeg!

Dr. Bea Wickett was a highly energetic woman whose political acuity and social grace was legendary and had no doubt helped her establish the finest school psychology department in North America. At the time I worked with her I was an inexperienced newly minted psychologist who was learning diplomacy at the hands of a master. One day one of my principals complained about the poor state of my shoes. As befits a family of lawyers I was ready for battle. Bea, demonstrating her superior social skills, managed to calm both parties down and to restore order.

Similarly I learned from Bea how to envision a program and, through the art of persuasion, political smarts and tenacity, make it happen. One such program implemented by this great lady is a counselling service for staff and teachers, a precursor of the many employee assistance programs currently available to teachers.

Today our company proudly provides employee assistance programs to many educational organizations.

With the full support of Bea, I sought and successfully became the chief psychologist of the Ottawa Civic Hospital, then a 1,000-bed teaching hospital associated with the University of Ottawa. Unknown to me at that time this was to be the pinnacle of my career with major consequences to my personal life.

During those initial months I was filled with anxiety and apprehension. The learning curve was challenging and filled with minefields that could literally destroy anyone's career. As I learned the inner workings of hospital management I realized that to be a player within the system one needed to be seen as visible and competent. Committee work, teaching and being available to senior management all formed part of my strategy to be visible in the hospital milieu.

While learning the inner workings of the hospital I met Dr. F, the senior medical executive officer. Dr. F was an old-fashioned type executive who literally knew everyone in the hospital. Walking with him down the corridors was a lesson in human dignity and respect as he greeted everyone by first name often inquiring about their family At Christmas he dressed up as Santa Claus visiting patients and staff alike.

Over the years I befriended Dr. F, I took the opportunity to eat lunch with him as often as possible to learn from him. I recall drawing up a list of needs for my department. Dr. F, like a father teaching his son, calmly and warmly responded that if a document was longer than a page it had no chance of being read. Thus began my real writing career as I struggled to present my thoughts and plans into a one-page executive summary.

The Psychology Division of the Department of Psychiatry, which I headed, was an archaic infrastructure that hindered the progress of psychology within the hospital and proved to be my most difficult political battle. Having received the blessings of the senior medical officer of the hospital to expand services, I was limited by the attitude of psychiatry that felt threatened by my stance. I faced an intense battle with both the hospital's department head and the chief psychiatrist of the University of Ottawa. At one point I was marched into the chief psychiatrist's office and told in no uncertain terms if I didn't stop my expansion of psychology he would remove all psychiatry residents from the hospital.

Those of you who know me realize that this was like waving a red flag in my face. My resolve to expand psychological services within the hospital and the community was reinforced by this autocratic and dictatorial behaviour. Of the many changes I made I am proudest of developing a psychology position with the cardiac rehabilitation program. In addition I hired, in association with the Department of Obstetrics and Gynaecology, the first psychologist in North America devoted exclusively to women's health issues.

Following my decision to return to private practice my personal life literally fell apart resulting in a mood of intense despair and depression. Somehow, despite my troubles, I was able to focus on my clients. I became a workaholic, serving direct with clients, marketing my services and generally learning the nuances of running a small business.

The first week I was in practice I had a huge break by agreeing to serve as the main Ottawa employment assistance programs provider for a large national company. Suddenly I had a stable income.

During the next 10 years I developed a highly successful practice that, combined with my teaching and consultation roles, provided me many challenges and a substantial income. I particularly enjoyed teaching at both the undergraduate and graduate level. After several years of teaching I was asked to teach the psychological assessment course at the University of Ottawa. I considered the offer an honour and I quickly immersed in it.

Students accepted into the PhD program represented *la crème de la crème*. Bright, articulate and ambitious they were eager to learn the tricks of the trades of their new career. I decided to do away with traditional marks in the interest of actually teaching them their craft. Their reaction shocked me. I was met with a wall of resistance. Despite their protests I persisted and all of them learned the basic necessities of their profession.

After several years my graduate teaching experience ended badly when it was taken away from me because of a policy decision not to offer graduate courses to part-time staff. This arbitrary decision soured my relations with the department and left a foul taste in my mouth.

Despite these challenges private practice was a perfect fit with my entrepreneurial and rebellious personality. It gave me the opportunity to pursue my own interests without being saddled with the burdens and politics of bureaucracy. I was once asked to apply for a senior position within the military but refused to be a candidate because the military brass would not allow me to exercise at lunchtime, a habit that had helped me cope with my many trials and tribulations over the years.

Psychology is a unique profession privy to a client's most intimate secrets. A non-judgmental attitude is essential. Most psychologists have their own prejudices and struggle with providing their clients with a safe, non-judgemental environment. It was often: "Dr. Nozick, what should I do about . . . ?" My consistent response was that I had enough problems in my life and did not want the responsibility of theirs. Clients, however, do impact on psychologists. After my divorce I made a special effort to try to repair marriages even though I could not save my own marriage.

On a personal basis I struggle on a daily basis not to be judgmental and impatient with my friends and family. With time and wisdom I have learned to lower my expectations of others and acknowledge the many blessings and gifts I have been given.

Despite this all psychologists are deeply affected by the way clients live and make decisions. I talked earlier about the many clients I admire for facing their demons. In many ways clients are like our own children. You try to provide them with the support and tools to grow and become contributing members of society. Not all clients, or for that matter children, proceed in a manner we choose or approve of, but as long as they make informed decisions it is their life to live.

I remember many years ago Greg told me I wanted him to be a lawyer or family doctor. My response: "I want you to be whatever you want, but if you're really asking my opinion I think you would make a great pediatrician." Like my clients, I have no right to influence either my clients or my children with my desires. I have lived my life and made my decisions. They are entitled to make theirs.

Despite my successes at that time I remain wanting in my private life. I preach balance to my clients but personally have none. I knew I wanted to become a better father, grandfather, friend, son or brother. Thus despite my financial success I turned my back on sole private practice and took advantage of an opportunity to join an established group practice.

At first my role was not clearly defined and I shared leadership of the practice with a young ambitious female psychologist. We tried to cooperate with each other but it didn't work for me. I needed to fly solo and to have the ultimate authority and control. After the dust settled I survived as the director. Currently I serve as a consultant and director of psychology to a large multi-health organization based in Toronto. I am now part of the cutting edge of private health care in Canada and by osmosis part of the on-going health care debate.

As a psychologist who has worked in both public and private sectors, I believe each has their merits. Combining the efficiency of the private sector with the willingness of the public sector to treat the most complicated cases offers a balanced approach.

Having returned to corporate Canada I have the luxury of being professionally autonomous and thus able to offer a highly ethical, professional and compassionate service to clients. For years I have made it part of my practice to offer services at a reduced rate to several clients who would not ordinary have access to the private sector.

At this stage of my career it is not about the money. My family will do just fine by themselves. When I am gone I hope that friends, family, clients, students and colleagues will continue to practise the life lessons I have tried to the best of my ability to live up to.

LIFE'S LESSON—*We can never repay our parents for what they have done for us. We pass down to our children and our children's children the goodness we owe our parents. Those without children pass it on to humanity in general and try to leave this world a better place for those who follow.*

CHAPTER 22

———— ✦ ————

A HEART PATIENT I AM

My friend, a fellow world traveller and physician, suggests I go in for my annual check-up that somehow I have managed to avoid for more than three years. A lifelong coward with regard to the medical system, I have always adopted a basic attitude. Why subjugate this wrinkly, liver-spotted, adipose enriched body to the humiliation of being probed and micro-analyzed to death?

Finally, after several aborted attempts, the dreaded event is scheduled for an early Friday morning well before my psychological defences are awake. Having earlier been told to get my blood level assessed, I did so. For those of you a little squeamish about the loss of blood I will not go into details how about how the blood is collected and given to some unknown analyst who is charged with giving you the verdict whether you have time to buy green bananas or not. Suffice to say that you are propelled into a chair, a noose tightened around your arm and then unceremoniously stabbed with a six-inch probe, sufficient to extract any fluid from the depths of your body Afterwards comes a cheery goodbye with a microscopic plaster (thank you daughter from South Africa) to hold back the tide of blood.

Next morning, after failing to negotiate the mile between my home and my doctor's office in a timely manner, I arrived five minutes late to find my doctor's office totally deserted by patients and staff alike. I was greeted by my friendly doctor's warm voice: "I'll be with you in a minute." Shortly, I'm ushered into his examining room and asked to strip to my essentials.

Following the usual medical history and examination (typical question is how many times do I get up to pee at night), I am asked to submit myself to one final indignity, the dreaded prostate test. For those of you who have experienced the exam no details are necessary. Those of you, who have not had the test, take it; it may save your life!

After reviewing my test results, my doctor tells me all is well but because of my age and family history, a stress test is advisable.

Two days later, as a result of a cancellation, I arrive at the world famous Heart Institute. I am shown into a large waiting room with fellow inmates where I am immediately exposed to truths and untruths about how they have been treated by the penal (medical) system.

Suddenly a disgustingly virile specimen of a man, who appears to have little empathy for the frail and elderly group I have recently joined, calls my name. I am ushered into a small room, with a window at eye level. A treadmill and gurney dominate the room with electric instruments strewn all over. Told to strip, I am fully prepared with my brand new swanky pale blue wash-and-wear shorts bought for the occasion. A razor shaves a 6x2 inch square area of my chest that took years for me to grow.

Electrodes are attached and suddenly the machine goes ballistics with sounds and sine waves going off everywhere. After order is restored, I am asked to walk then run as the platform is elevated to where I can barely stand, thereby stressing my heart to the maximum for the purpose of acquiring new sine waves that somehow will measure my health. As I struggle to cope with these enormous demands, I look out that little window where I see ordinary life taking place. This sharp contrast to the surreal situation I find myself in helps me to slowly return to the world of the living.

I ask the technician how I did. Against all the rules he tells me that I had a positive test and will need further testing thereby raising my blood pressure even higher.

I leave the testing devastated, barely able to walk under my now malfunctioning heart. Awaiting the results of the test I hope against hope that a real cardiologist will reverse the verdict. After further consultation with my friend and doctor I am told that because of my family history (Russian Jewish genes no less), I will need further testing to rule out cardiac problems. Thus began my introduction to the cardiac world.

After an anguishing three-week wait, I once again enter the diagnostic wing of the Heart Institute, not as staff or director of psychology, but like my peers as a simple, humble and scared patient. When met by the same technician who had previously tested me my anxiety rises to another level. Following the same procedure, with the addition of an inserted radio-active dye, I duly perform the stress test followed by a quick hop on a gurney to a near-by camera that takes detailed pictures of the blood flow to my heart.

Afraid to directly ask the technician the results, I perceive (I am after all a psychologist) a subtle hint that all is not well.

After another lengthy wait my doctor tells me that the test results show some abnormalities of minor concern. Downplaying the results after further consultation with a cardiologist he suggests I go on medicine to lower my blood pressure and cholesterol count.

A highly anxious person, who has battled anxiety and control all my life, I now become like my father before me a cardiac patient dependent on medication for survival. My mind in overdrive projects scenarios ranging from immediate death to a minor inconvenience.

Finally David, the professional, restores order and control by asking my doctor to refer me to a cardiologist at the world famous Heart Institute. In the interim I let go of my bias against drugs and agree to take the medicine prescribed me.

What follows are weekly visits to my family doctor in consort with regular blood tests to monitor the flow, intensity, and contents of my blood. I am reduced to crazy numbers of mmolL cholesterol, triglycerides, HDL cholesterol, LDL cholesterol, TC/HDL C Ratio with target goals set at even more crazy numbers.

After another lengthy wait, I arrive yet again at the second floor of the world famous Heart Institute. I am duly registered and issued my own green card identifying me as a cardiac patient, a designation I have fought all my life to avoid.

Efficiently and effortlessly blood is taken, my heart monitored and before I know it I appear before Dr. L, my esteemed cardiologist. After a physical exam he carefully and expertly explains the abnormalities in my test results. It seems I might have a heart value or blockage issue and further tests are needed.

I leave devastated and in shock, convinced I am my father's child. Somehow, without experiencing one single symptom, I have officially become a heart patient in need of the health care system. CT scans and an echo ultrasound follow as I proceed further into the world of the heart patient. After one test is abruptly stopped before pictures can be taken I know I am in trouble. Indeed, not five minutes after I return home I receive an ominous call from my cardiologist that he wants to perform an angiogram to examine if my arteries are blocked. Panic and fear reach levels heretofore unknown to me. I become my own worst patient unable to concentrate or focus on what must be done. Finally I talk myself down utilizing the skill set I know I have. I put a plan into action. I find others who have gone through this daunting test. Many are negative and morose. I notify family and relatives and, preparing for the worst, rewrite my will.

Suddenly, in the middle of a sun-drenched Ottawa afternoon comes divine intervention. I receive a telephone call from an old friend whom I have had little contact in recent years but whom I previously enjoyed a close and warm bond. A former seminarian, I tell Len about my health issues and he immediately informs me he went through the exact same predicament and test some 15 years earlier with a successful outcome. Indeed he is living proof. All is well!

Len is the antidote to the negative and dismal talk I have heard from others. Indeed his calm reassurance is what I need to calm my frayed nerves. He relays his symptoms, test results and emotions that miraculously correspond exactly to my own. He soothes my nerves and restores order and balance to my soul.

As I await the angiogram I oscillate between fear and calmness, try to let go of control and accept whatever fate has prescribed. I am told I do indeed have modest coronary heart disease. Currently I am attending the brief program of the Cardiac Rehabilitation Unit and am committed to changing my diet and exercise regimes. I remain a work in progress and hope to survive to a ripe old age using the lessons I articulate in this manuscript.

LIFE'S LESSON—*Live each day as if it is your last.*

CHAPTER 23

LESSONS LEARNED

All people age. With age comes wisdom if you are lucky and open to life experience.

Wisdom is learning to make appropriate social and moral judgments as a result of learning from life's mistakes. Only the wise acknowledge and learn from their mistakes.

Lucky for me, early in my career I was assigned to the same notorious high school as Bill, an attendance officer and social worker. Bill, who rose to be the board's chief social worker, was a man who knew how to relate to troubled adolescents and their families. He was respectful but firm. Unfortunately, we lost this kind warrior many years too early.

Essentially what Bill demonstrated to me was to believe in oneself, to be true to one's core values and to be authentic and real. As the name of this manuscript implies you cannot please all the people all the time but if you are true to yourself you will be respected and valued. Teenagers have the uncanny ability to smell out the bullshit and to ignore adults who lecture or judge them.

In addition to my clinical and administrative roles, I highly valued my opportunity to teach. During one such occasion I was teaching an undergraduate psychology course at Carleton University, whose faculty of psychology was primarily experimental. Following completion of the course the students evaluated the professor. In this instance I received two opinions from two different students that made me take note. In one case I was told I was the worst professor he ever had. Remarkably another student in the same class rated me as the best professor he ever had.

How does one evaluate these vastly different opinions? It seems that teaching the course in a clinical manner found one student aversive and another admiring. The lesson to be learned is the importance of filtering feedback and communication. No matter what anybody says it is extremely important to decide yourself if they makes sense. I have tried to communicate to every one of my clients the importance of filtering opinions of others, a lesson all of us would do well to remember.

In addition to filtering opinions and relying on one's own judgment one principle I attempt to follow in my own life is to concentrate on the process and not the outcome. In any situation you can only give it your best shot. No one can predict what will actually happen. Professional golfers have a mantra for this concept they call playing one shot at a time. I recently took in a documentary featuring the *Young@Heart* chorus in which the filmmaker followed the life of senior choir members as they readied for a major concert tour in Europe. This highly acclaimed choir under the direction of Bob Cilman has travelled the world entertaining young and old. The camera captures the personal struggles and efforts many of the choir members have to overcome to perform.

There is one especially emotional scene in which the soloist requires oxygen to continue. The choir demonstrates a concept that is critical to one's inner peace, namely that we have little control of our destiny or the external world. It seems these wise choir members intuitively realize that life is lived one moment at a time and that no one can foresee the future. Their passion in living life one moment at a time is a valuable lesson to us all.

Many of my clients suffered either from not having a self-identity or not being a part of something bigger than themselves.

Readers will recall that on one of my visits to Israel I spent rewarding days visiting a kibbutz in the Western Negev. This was an English-speaking kibbutz where my son spent a fulfilling year of his life. Kibbutzim is defined by all members as being treated equally. While visiting, I met Mira, internationally known and struggling to be accepted as an artist. The kibbutz council did not approve of her work and wanted her to make a different contribution to the kibbutz. In this instance the power of the community took precedence over self-identity.

It seems in Western society that community only counts when there is a crisis such as recent hurricanes, floods or snowstorms where survival itself may depend on the kindness of neighbours. A good example of this was the small community of Gander, Newfoundland, that took in strangers to their homes when North American skies where closed as a result of the events of 9/11. Their generosity enabled many Americans to develop life-long friendships with their hosts in Gander.

A healthy adult learns to balance self-identity with the need to be part of a community. Kibbutzim, founded on the principles of Karl Marx, do wonders for developing a sense of community but little to enhance self-identity. The stronger one's self-identity the more difficult it is to accept one's community role.

On the other hand it is a very lonely person who lives only for himself. Volunteer work and community service are all ways of being part of a community. The engaging aging choir I described earlier demonstrates a passion and a strong sense of community that literally defies death.

Life's lessons or personal growth can occur only when one goes out of their comfort zone. Unfortunately we all seek security and thus, more often than not, events occur that serve to dislodge us from our complacency before personal growth is possible.

In the process of recovering from a divorce that shook me to my foundation, I learned a valuable lesson in life. Namely, in order to receive emotional support it is necessary to tell others of your pain and suffering. In addition to reaching out to others it is important to have mentors or others whom you respect, to seek wise advice and counsel when one is lost as I was at that point in my life. No man is an island. We all need help and assistance from time to time.

Recently I moved into a condominium where many seniors reside. Getting to know them has allowed me access to their considerable life experiences. Just last week I learned from my bridge partner the real history of the National Hockey League, his grandfather being one of the original owners. When I was the Director of Psychology at a major teaching hospital in Ottawa, I recall supervising three PhD candidates. I asked them: "Why am I sitting behind this desk?" After 10 seconds of silence I told them: "Despite the fact that you are smarter, better looking and richer the only reason I am sitting behind the desk is I have more life experience than you."

Life experience means at some level you are a survivor of life's challenges. You are alive and kicking despite what you had to endure. Being alive means you are privileged to experience life and no one knows what lies ahead. Earlier I also told you of the trials and tribulations of Louise, who was at times so traumatized and fragile that it was not at all certain she would make it across the minefield. At times my only advice to her was to take life one moment at a time. No one knew what tomorrow would bring. There was always hope life would become better.

Perhaps one of the most valuable lessons in life is to live your life to the fullest every day. Each of us must decide what that means to us. To me it means taking advantage of life's opportunities, whether to travel to South Africa where my children spent a parental leave, to stretching myself professionally to take on difficult and complicated cases, or pursuing my dream of finding my true soul mate despite the pain, disappointment and sadness that often results. To live life to the fullest means coping with failures before success comes. It means being passionate and involved in the world's problems, being informed and educated about the issues of the day. It means reaching for the impossible dream that we together will leave this world a better place for our children and our children's children.

In concluding my thoughts I refer to *The Mishna,* edited by Rabbi Judah. *The Prince in the year 200 of the Common Era* is the first major text containing the views of rabbinic scholars on the Torah (the five books of Moses) and is generally considered the foundation of Judaism. Within the *Mishna* is a section known as *Ethics of the Fathers,* which provides insights and maxims on how to be a good Jew, a *mentsch* (an honourable man). "Who is strong?" it asks. "He who subdues his personal inclinations."

My mentor Mo said the same thing in a different way. "You learn to seek happiness by limiting desires, rather than in attempting to satisfy them."

What does it mean to limit one's appetite in order to reach a state of happiness? It seems less is more. It is not from our yearnings or desires that we receive pleasure but more from appreciating our blessings. A happy contented man is a man who appreciates his blessings and his lot in life.

LIFE'S LESSON—*This whole chapter summarizes life's lesson.*

CHAPTER 24

REFLECTIONS ON BEING 65

I am now officially a senior citizen. Following my tradition with any major happening I went on a long run in the windy, snowy Ottawa winter partly to show I am alive and partly to defy the aging process. I rejoice that I can still do it.

What does it mean to me to be 65? Officially I am starting the aging process but, with the exception of this medical matter I need to attend to, I do not feel old either in body or spirit. I heard a wonderful saying the other day from a close medical friend who recently retired. At this stage of life he feels he has "a lot of wisdom but little knowledge." During a recent rabbinical lecture the Rabbi offered an off the cuff remark that resonated with me. "Intelligent people talk about ideas, less intelligent people talk about other people."

Certainty I feel blessed with good health, a warm and loving family, and many close friendships. I am still able to practise and enjoy my craft and feel a fully functioning member of society. I am aware that as I age I face limitations and loss of functioning that will challenge me down the road. The recent heart procedure and the effect it may or may not have on my life qualify as challenges. I am hopeful that prayer, professional competency and the support of my friends and family will help me overcome these challenges.

I have learned to appreciate my blessings and to avoid toxic people and situations that serve to only drain energy. There are many people out there who simply do not get it. I try as much as humanly possible to surround myself with people who not only talk the talk but, more importantly, walk the walk. These people fill me with love, compassion, respect and dignity. I am grateful for their presence in my life.

Recently I have chosen to renew my search for a life partner, no easy task for a man who by choice or happenstance has lived much of his adult life alone. I look for guidance from above on this life altering decision. I have renewed my desire to continue practising my craft as well as assuming the added responsibility of serving as a consultant to a national organization. Having reached the age of wisdom, I am attempting to apply this to the workplace. As long as my good health prevails I have no plans for retirement and feel blessed to find my work both a pleasure and a passion. I hope to continue my world travels and see firsthand the miracles of this earth.

Lastly, it is my desire to complete this written document. It has been a long arduous project with many detours but the finishing line is approaching.

LIFE'S LESSON—Life is a journey that is best lived one day, one moment at a time. Stop, listen with compassion and without prejudice, touch with the curiosity of a newborn, feel with the passion of the beating heart, and above all be your brother's keeper and you will experience a life of meaning and joy. Lastly in the words of my mentor Mo: "Illegitimi Non Carborundum_Don't let the Bastards Wear You Down".